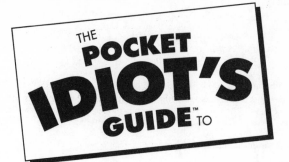

Copyrights

by Robert J. Frohwein and Gregory Scott Smith

D1517618

A member of Penguin Group (USA) Inc.

To our wives, Dana and Laura, and our children, Michael, Lizabeth and Scott, who put up with us as we spent our nights and weekends writing this book.

Contents

Appendixes

Introduction

TVs, cars, furniture, and clothes. It's relatively easy to identify and understand who owns these types of items because they can be touched and felt. However, certain things you own can't be touched in the same way as your television set, car, furniture, or clothes. This kind of property is called *intellectual property*. The reason for its name? It's stuff that is developed with your mind.

While it's easy to know who owns the car parked in your driveway, it's a bit more difficult to see intellectual property and then figure out who owns it! Because it's difficult to see, it's also difficult to stop folks from stealing it. As a result, laws have been developed over the years to protect intellectual property.

In this book, we'll introduce you to one category of intellectual property known as *copyrights*. We'll do this by explaining what can be and what can't be protected by copyrights, how to make sure your work is protected, and how to keep out of trouble with others' copyrights. We'll also help you understand some of the pluses and minuses associated with copyright ownership.

Extras to Help You Along

This book also has useful information provided in sidebars throughout the text.

Straight from the Record

This box contains fascinating stories about the history of copyrights.

Objections

This box provides cautions that will keep you inside the boundaries of the law.

Good Counsel

This box has simple tips to help you recognize and protect your intellectual property.

Proper Pointers

These boxes boil down legalese into easy-to-understand language.

Acknowledgments

We'd like to thank Paul Dinas, Michael Koch, Billy Fields, Anja Mutic, and everyone else from Alpha Books for their help in finalizing the book.

About the Authors

Robert J. Frohwein is the founder and CEO of LAVA Group, Inc. and a partner with LAVA Group Law, LLC, both headquartered in Atlanta, Georgia; both firms provide services to companies nationwide. Collectively, the two firms are the first to help clients throughout the lifecycle of intellectual property—that is helping companies innovate, protect, and leverage intellectual property. Learn more at www.lavagroup.net. Rob formerly held senior business and legal executive positions with several technology firms and practiced as an intellectual property and corporate attorney with a large, international law firm. Rob is married to Dana and has two children, Michael and Lizabeth. Rob can be reached at rfrohwein@lavagroup.net.

Gregory Scott Smith focuses in his legal practice on technology clients. He used to be a partner at one of the largest international firms based in Atlanta and prior to that, he was with the law firm of Jones & Askew. Gregory spent 14 years as an engineer working for the National Security Agency, Georgia Tech Research Institute, and Panasonic. At Panasonic, Gregory headed up the software group of their cellular telephone division. Gregory has a Bachelor degree in engineering from Western Kentucky University, a Masters in engineering from George Washington University, and a law degree from Georgia State. He is a partner and co-founder of LAVA Group Law by Smith & Frohwein and co-owner of LAVA Group, Inc. Gregory is married to Laura and has a son Scott. Gregory can be reached at gsmith@lavagroup.net.

Trademarks

All terms mentioned in this book that are known to be or are suspected of being trademarks or service marks have been appropriately capitalized. Alpha Books and Penguin Group (USA) Inc. cannot attest to the accuracy of this information. Use of a term in this book should not be regarded as affecting the validity of any trademark or service mark.

Chapter 1

Copyright or Copy Wrong?

In This Chapter

- Getting comfortable with copyrights
- The basic rules of copyright
- How is it different from patents and trademarks?

If you're seen walking down the street carrying someone else's TV, it's difficult to convince the police that you didn't know the TV belonged to someone else. Similarly, the law doesn't give you a break for stealing someone else's copyright (known as *infringement*) just because you say you didn't know it belonged to someone else. Therefore, one of the first and most important things is to learn how to identify something that is or can be *copyrighted*.

Copyrights are only one form of intellectual property protection. Other types of intellectual property protection include patents, trademarks, and trade secrets. Each of these is meant to apply to different things and provide different types of coverage.

In this chapter, we discuss the very basics of a copyright. We also briefly explain the differences between copyrights and patents, trademarks, and trade secrets.

What Is a Copyright?

A copyright is a type of legal protection provided by each state in the United States and also by the U.S. federal government. The U.S. copyright law states that "copyright protection subsists ... in original works of authorship fixed in any tangible medium of expression ... from which they can be perceived, reproduced, or otherwise communicated ...."

Uggh, what does all that legal speak mean?! It means there are certain types of works that are protected under certain circumstances. We'll break that confusing definition into a few simple parts: works, originality, and recordation (otherwise known as *fixed in a tangible medium*).

> **Straight from the Record**
>
> The U.S. Constitution provides the United States Congress with the authority to pass laws that, for a *limited time*, protect *writings* to "promote the progress of science and useful arts."

Works

We keep using the term *works*. But what is a work? It is the subject matter that can be copyrighted. As you'll find out later, we describe nearly all the things that the government decided should be considered *works*. For now, you can generally think of them as books, newspapers, magazines, music, computer software, artwork, and plays. In fact, the official categories that the U.S. Copyright Office protects are: literary works (for example, a book), performing arts works (such as a play), sound recordings (such as a song), serials and periodicals (such as a newspaper), and visual arts (for example, a painting).

We'll go into great detail on each of these areas so that you can quickly figure out what kind of work you're curious about. This will help you determine whether you already have copyright protection and if not, whether you can register your work. To keep it simple, we call all of these items works throughout this book.

Originality

We mentioned earlier that a work must be original in order to be copyrighted. If you make a photocopy of this page of this book, you have not created anything original—you simply copied the words that we have written. However, if you read this book and write a book report about it, then congrats! You've written something original, even though you were inspired by someone else's efforts.

Basically, the original aspects of a work can be copyrighted. Therefore, if you take someone else's song and add a new ending to it, you won't have a copyright in the original song, but only in the portion that you created. The amazing thing is that even a tiny bit of creativity and originality is pretty much all you need.

The creativity doesn't even have to be something altogether new. It can take the form of the way in which you arrange other people's efforts. A good example of this might be a coffee-table book of headlines from various newspapers from the time of the Civil War. While the person collecting and arranging these headlines didn't publish the newspaper, he or she can have a copyright in the compiled effort. What was original about this? It was the unique way of arranging the headlines.

Recordation

We've discussed works and originality. The final requirement of copyright is *recordation*. The U.S. Copyright Office refers to recordation as a work "being fixed in a tangible medium." This essentially means that the work is either written down, recorded, or otherwise accessible after the date it was created. Oftentimes, confusion regarding the concept of recordation creeps in when you consider events or performances, like a rock concert at a local hall, a baseball game at the Yankee Stadium, or a chess match in a convention hall. Suppose the rock band at the local hall comes up with an impromptu song while performing. Would that rock band have any rights in the new song? Or could some aspiring musician in the audience listen to the song, go home, record and release it (and make a fortune)?

Surprisingly, the answer used to be that the aspiring musician could make a fortune off of it. The reason? The song was never recorded—it was simply played for the crowd. Under copyright law, the band would have needed to record their concert to have rights. However, Congress passed a law called the Uruguay Round Agreements Act to prevent the aspiring musician from exploiting the song and making a fortune.

Objections

We're not recommending that you bring a tape recorder into the next rock concert that you attend. Taping a concert is considered a violation of the Uruguay Round Agreements Act, which precludes the unauthorized recording of live musical performances.

What Constitutes Recordation?

Why is it so important that a work be recorded? In the absence of recordation, it's difficult to establish what exactly was created. Nobody wants to get into a battle of memories! Therefore, the medium that you use to record the work is key. This medium must allow someone to *perceive* (for example, a work written on paper), *reproduce* (for example, making a photocopy of paper), or *communicate* (for example, playing a music CD in a CD player) the work.

The following list itemizes some examples of a tangible medium for recording a work:

- An audiotape or videotape
- A flash memory card
- A notebook
- A hard disk drive of a computer
- Scrap paper, a napkin, a beer mat, and so on

The following items are not a tangible medium:

- Your memory
- The FCC's frequencies
- Your eyes
- The sand on a beach

Good Counsel

Make sure you write down your words or music! Remember, copyrights must be recorded. Write down or record your great stories, song lyrics, and historic air guitar performance. Or someone else may!

A Couple of Need-to-Knows

You're nearly ready to be a self-proclaimed expert of what can be protected by copyright, but not quite yet! There are a couple of other things to keep in the back of your mind when reviewing items for copyright protection—the concepts of *expression* and *publication*.

Express Yourself!

A basic principle of copyrights is that they protect the expression of an idea, not the idea itself. Expression is the unique way in which you present information, perform a play, write a song, or provide your opinion on a topic. Therefore, if you've just invented the flying car, copyright laws will not protect your idea (see the short description on patents later in this chapter). However, if you write a story about an inventor who comes up with a new invention—the flying car—your story would be protected by copyright.

The concept of expression versus an idea can be a bit tricky. A single idea can be expressed in more than one way. A good example comes from the world of music. In his hit "Daniel," Elton John wrote about Daniel leaving on a plane. Similarly, John Denver wrote a hit called "Leaving on a Jet Plane." Although both songs talk about similar ideas, the manner in which they express these ideas is different. Therefore, a distinctly separate copyright attaches to each of the two songs.

Do I Need to Publish the Work?

A common myth is that a work needs to be published to be protected by the copyright law. Publication, which generally means that a work is copied and distributed to the public for sale, is *not* a requirement of copyright law.

This being said, publication can affect your rights as a copyright holder, in terms of the rules regarding registration and the longevity of a copyright.

What's Not a Copyright?

As you have seen in the previous sections, there are only a few requirements for something to be protected by the copyright law. These relatively simple steps sometimes make people think that almost everything is or should be covered by copyright law. Don't fall into that trap! We provide you with a couple of key examples of what we call "copywrongs"—items that are commonly thought to be covered by copyright law, but are actually not covered.

Short Stuff

Short "writings"—such as titles, names, short phrases, slogans, familiar symbols or designs, lettering, coloring, and mere listings of ingredients or contents—cannot be copyrighted. Here are some examples of items that are not protected by copyright law:

- Just Do It!® —This is a Nike®, Inc. registered trademark.
- © —The copyright symbol cannot, in itself, be copyrighted.
- The ingredients of Campbell's® chicken soup.
- Mr., Mrs., Dr., or Ph.D.
- The color brown.

However, some of these items may be protected as trademarks, as we'll discuss shortly.

Ideas and Such

The following items also cannot be protected by copyright law: ideas, procedures, methods, systems, processes, concepts, principles, discoveries, or devices. That is because they're abstract concepts. In fact, they may be better protected by patent law (see our discussion of patents below). However, a description, explanation, or an illustration of any one of the foregoing items can be copyrighted because it is an example of expression (that is, the unique way they're communicated).

It's Only Natural!

Works that contain *no originality* are not protected by copyrights. Examples include formulas ($E=mc^2$), standard calendars, rulers, scientific tables, and the like. Recognize, though, that you can take a standard calendar and combine it with some originality (for example, you can include cartoons, pictures, or graphics) to create an original work that is subject to copyright protection. Thus, a Dilbert® calendar can be protected through copyright.

You Decide!

As a quick review, we want to provide you with several examples of different works and explain why they can or cannot be protected by copyrights (remember, they must be *original* and *recorded*):

- Your new self-portrait: Yes, because it's original and *recorded* on a canvass that can be copied and distributed to others.

- A photograph of this book's cover: No, because the cover of this book was created by someone else and your picture is nothing more than a direct copy of someone else's copyrighted work.

- The hopscotch court you drew on your driveway: No, for a couple of reasons. First, the hopscotch court may not be original, unless you've drawn the court in some unique way. The other issue is whether the court is really recorded. Sidewalk chalk, given the fact that it can be washed away with water (rain), may not meet the recordation requirement because it is not considered fixed.

- The printing of the periodic table of elements on the back of your business card: No, this is not protectable because this table would be considered a scientific table not subject to copyright protection.

- Your daughter's school play: No, unless you tape the play. If you tape it, the unique way in which your daughter's group performs the play would be protected.

- An interpretive depiction of the Mona Lisa: Yes, the unique interpretive aspects would be protected (for example, if you use a new color arrangement for the painting). You could not claim protection, though, in the original painting or even, perhaps, someone else's interpretation (just as long as they didn't copy yours).

They're Not Patents or Trademarks!

Many people lump patents, trademarks, and copyrights together. While they all have one thing in common (they're all forms of *intellectual property*), they are not the same and should not be used interchangeably. Each is a different form of legal protection covering items created by your mind.

We want to provide you with a quick description of what patents and trademarks protect so that you can forever tell them apart.

Patents

Unlike a copyright, which protects works, a patent is a form of legal protection for ideas, inventions, processes, and methods. Your article about a new idea can be protected by a copyright, but the idea itself can be protected with a patent. Unlike with a copyright, your invention is not protected the moment you conceive it and put it down on paper. Rather, you must go through the process of applying for a patent through the U.S. Patent and Trademark Office.

Patent protection enables the patent owner to prevent others from doing certain things with the invention. Specifically, the patent owner can prevent others from making, using, selling, offering to sell, or importing products or services that are covered by the patent. Essentially, the grant gives the inventor a monopoly in the invention for a limited period of time (while the patent is in force).

Trademarks

Trademarks protect those words and symbols (called *marks*) that help consumers identify the origin of the goods. These marks typically act as the *brands* a company may use to offer its products or services. For example, the name *Coke* identifies a drink sold by the Coca Cola Company. Trademarks are also associated with a defined set of products or services, or both. Therefore, a mark that covers the distribution of sink faucets may be the same as a mark that covers airline services (for example, Delta).

Trademark protection allows the trademark owner to prohibit others from using a mark that is confusingly similar. If a person or company is using a mark that is too similar to a registered trademark, that mark may be found to be infringing the registered mark. As an example, a red beverage aluminum can with *Coco Cola* scripted on the side would be found to be confusingly similar and therefore infringing the Coca Cola trademark.

Good Counsel _____

Your strategy should be to seek to protect your company through a combination of intellectual properties—patent, trademarks, copyrights, and trade secrets.

The Least You Need to Know

- Copyrights only cover original material; copies of someone else's original work are not protected by copyright.

- To possess a copyright, your work must be recorded.

- Titles, slogans, ideas, and symbols are some of the items that cannot be protected by copyright law.

- Generally, patents protect inventions, trademarks protect names, and brands and copyrights protect expressive works.

Chapter 2

Types of Works

In This Chapter

- Identifying different types of works
- Examples of each type of work
- Detailed explanations of certain works

We've discussed the criteria for whether something can be protected by the copyright law. Now we delve into some detail regarding the different types of works that are protected by copyright.

Although the U.S. Constitution used the word "writings" to describe what can be protected by copyright law, Congress has enacted laws that define this in a much broader sense than you would have imagined. When the Constitution provided authority to protect writings, pretty much all that existed were physical writings and objects (such as books, paintings, and sculptures). During that era you could not record a concert on a tape or save a program to the hard disk of a computer.

Technology not only expanded the realm of works that needed to be protected, but also increased the likelihood of infringement. Digital files are readily sent via e-mail, and wireless technologies enable access into computer networks. Therefore, while you read about the different types of works that are protected, you should recognize that this list has changed over the years and may likely change again in the future to meet the needs of our ever-changing technological society.

Types of Works and the Reasons You Should Care

As we discussed, copyrights fall into one of a variety of categories:

- Literary works
- Visual arts works
- Performing arts works
- Sound recordings
- Serials and periodicals

It's important to classify your work in order to ensure it is subject to copyright protection. It's also important, as we explain later, to choose the proper federal registration form. We take you through each of the categories so you can decide which one of them your own work falls into.

Literary Works

Quite simply, literary works are expressed in words, numbers, or other verbal manners (for example, symbols). A literary work can be recorded on paper, computer disc, or some other physical form. Even if a literary work is not in a traditional format that does not change the fact that it is still a literary work. Please keep in mind that a copyright doesn't protect the ideas contained in a literary work, such as a book.

The underlying facts in a book or their various inter-pretations are not protected by copyright. For ex-ample, if you write a book on a new theory about who shot JFK, your theory could be used by another person in a different book and you could not claim copyright infringement. Good examples of literary works include books, online works (the articles you post on your website), poetry, computer programs, other printed materials (like pamphlets, tests, and reports), or other texts. Regardless of the subject and the medium of the work—whether it's fiction or nonfiction, in a tangible book or on the hard disk of your computer—it will still be considered a literary work. And you never thought you would be considered a literary author!

The following list provides various examples of lit-erary works. Although not exhaustive, it demonstrates the range of items that fall into the literary works category.

Examples of literary works include:

- Fiction, nonfiction, poetry, single pages of text
- Computer programs, games, automated databases
- Contributions to a collection, compilations
- Speeches, manuscripts, reports
- Dissertations, theses
- Bound or loose-leaf volumes
- Reference books, directories
- Brochures, pamphlets, catalogs, advertising copy
- Online works
- Textbooks

Some of the examples above need further explanation.

Compilations

A *compilation* is pretty much what you would think—a group of information borrowed from various sources but put together in such a way that the final product as a whole can be considered original and creative. A good example of a compilation is a book of great headlines about World War II gathered from newspapers all around the country. They can be arranged in such a way that the collection has its own original message.

Collective Works

A *collective work* is a collection of individual pieces that makes up a final product. A good example of a collective work is a magazine that includes multiple articles. The aspects that are protected by copyright include your original efforts to revise, edit, and compile the work and make it fit for publishing.

Now, what's the difference between a compilation and a collective work? A compilation is only one aspect of the effort that goes into creating a collective work. A collective work assumes that you also need to do some editing and revising. As a result, you not only have a copyright in the unique way in which you put it together (or compiled it) but also in the edited and revised aspects of the work.

Online Works

In its simplest form, an *online work* is information presented online, such as the data on the home page of a website. The copyright only extends to those aspects of the work that are otherwise copyrightable. This means, for example, that a particular color scheme that you have on your website is not subject to copyright protection. You'll need to clearly identify what is and what is not copyrightable when you apply for copyright registration. The other issue with online works is that websites are updated very frequently. Unfortunately, if you want to register for a copyright every time you update your site, you'll need to register each update separately (and, of course, pay a separate fee each time!).

Games

Aspects of games that contain what is considered literary or pictorial expression can be protected by copyright. For example, the aspects of the game Monopoly protected by copyright might be the rules, the playing pieces (after all, they're miniature sculptures, right?) and the arrangement of the streets around the board. All of these aspects fall under the literary works category (even though a sculpture is considered a visual arts work).

Poetry

If you're an aspiring poet, your works fall under the literary works category. In fact, if you published a collection of your poetry, you can register the entire collection in one fell swoop for one fee! The rules for unpublished works are a bit different. Essentially, you are safe to register your entire collection as long as you were the only person involved in developing and compiling your efforts and you've done so in an orderly fashion under a single title. If others were involved in the development of the work you want to file, you should refer to the specific rules regarding copyrighting poetry; you can find the rules at www.copyright.gov. The nice thing about this approach is that with a single effort, you effectively protected the entire collection of poems.

Computer Programs

Computer programs are also considered literary works (and you never thought of Bill Gates as the author of a literary work!). As you most likely know, computer programs are made up of source code, otherwise known as a set of instructions interpreted by a computer to take certain actions and create a desired result. Once again, a copyright will only protect the way you wrote the program. Another person can develop a computer program that performs similar tasks and produces the same result. However, as long as that person didn't write the source code substantially similar to yours, he or she did not infringe on your copyright.

Visual Arts

Visual arts works include many of the items that you might imagine—paintings, sculptures, and drawings. Some of the other examples, such as jewelry designs and dolls, may not be so obvious. A visual arts work can be two-dimensional (a picture) or three-dimensional (a sculpture); it can also be fine, graphic, or applied art. Interestingly, architectural drawings also fall into this category. Can you obtain a copyright in your sighting of an alien spaceship? The answer is no, but you can claim a visual arts copyright in your photograph of the historic sighting (and likely sell it for a good sum!).

Examples of visual arts works include:

- Photographs, drawings, paintings, murals
- Games, puzzles
- Greeting cards, postcards, stationary
- Jewelry designs

- Dolls, toys
- Artificial flowers and plants
- Artwork on clothing
- Advertisements, commercial prints, labels
- Bumper stickers, decals, stickers
- Cartoons, comic strips
- Posters, reproductions such as lithographs
- Needlework and craft kits, patterns for sewing and knitting
- Fabric, floor, and wall-covering designs
- CD jacket artwork and photography
- Sculptures such as carvings, ceramics, and figurines
- Architectural drawings or plans, blueprints, and diagrams

Useful Articles

Some visual arts works are considered *useful articles*, which means that they do more than simply communicate the information that could be protected by copyright. For example, the china you received as a wedding present has a design that can be protected by copyright as a visual arts work. However, it's also useful in that you eat off of it! The portion of the useful article that would be protected is the visually distinctive aspect (for example, the flower pattern on the plate). However, copyrights do not protect the useful aspect (you can't stop others from making plates).

Good Counsel

Some designs can also be protected under patent law by what is called a design patent.

Performing Arts Works

Performing arts works are works that are intended to be performed in front of an audience (either live or through an outlet like a TV or in a movie theatre). Performing arts works include:

- Dramatic works, such as movie scripts (complete with the soundtrack)
- Musical works, such as concerts
- Movies and other audiovisual works
- Dance routines (choreographic works), including performances in operas, Broadway musicals or plays, ballets, or motion pictures

Performing arts works can sometimes be confused with a visual arts work, the underlying literary work, or a musical recording so make sure you know what exactly you're seeking to protect.

Special Considerations for Scripts

It would be easy to think that a movie, TV, or theater script should fall into the literary work category because it's textual. The key thing to remember with a script or similar type of writing (such as a screenplay) is that it is intended to be performed and therefore considered a performing arts work.

Some of the factors that influence this in the writings are cues for plot and directions for action. Once again, the general idea behind a performing arts work (for example, the general subject of a movie script) cannot be protected by copyright.

Sound Recordings

You're probably saying, "I don't need an explanation of this one!" It sounds pretty obvious, but has a few tricks to it. This category includes works that have a series of spoken, musical, or other types of sound. However, musical efforts that go along with a movie or other type of audiovisual work are excluded from this category; those fall into the performing arts category. Some good examples are recordings of a professor's lecture or The Beatles album "Let It Be."

The key here is that these recordings are strictly focused on the recordation of sound rather than audiovisuals recorded on a videotape. All of the CDs in your collection are sound recordings (unless they are from a movie soundtrack) and, if they were bought in a reputable store, should contain a copyright notice. Your copyright in a sound recording will cover both the performance and the manner in which the performance was engineered and produced. The current big issue in the music recording industry is that many people are ignoring the copyrights for these types of works and simply downloading them illegally from websites or from their peers.

Also, a related work may fall into more than one category and you may need to register it in each of the relevant categories. Here's an example. A writer writes a song. If the writer decides to register this song, he or she should register it as a performing arts work (because it is intended to be performed). If the same writer now performs and records only the sound of that song, then he or she may register the efforts as follows: the song composition as a performing arts work and the recorded song as a sound recording, *or* both together as a sound recording. If a different person performs the song, then the writer of the song can register the musical composition as a performing arts work and the performer can register the recording as a sound recording.

Serials and Periodicals

Works that are intended to be issued in successive parts with an indication of where it falls in the series (like a monthly magazine with the month and year on the cover) are considered *serials*. Good examples of serials and periodicals include newspapers, magazines, or other similar works that are delivered or provided on a regular basis. The morning paper is the best example of this type of work.

The Least You Need to Know

- Copyrights fall into one of five subject matter categories.
- Works protected by copyright include written works, songs, movies, computer programs, artwork, and many others.
- For registration, rights, and duration purposes, it's important to understand which category your work falls into.

Chapter 3

Copyrights: Your Rights and Theirs

In This Chapter

- Your exclusive rights as copyright owner
- Crossing the line: copyright infringement
- Transferring copyrights

Now it's time to understand what all this copyright fuss is about. If you own a copyright in a work, what benefits do you really get?

Typically, copyright owners are concerned about others reaping the benefit of the hard work that went into creating the copyrighted work. However, most people don't understand to which extent they're protected by copyright law and how to handle other people's copyrighted works.

In this chapter, you learn about each exclusive right of a copyright holder, what copyright infringement is and how you can avoid it (or detect others who are infringing), and how to license or sell your copyrighted work.

Rights of the Copyright Holder

Congrats! As a copyright owner, you will enjoy five exclusive rights when it comes to your copyrighted work. Why should you care? Exclusivity means that you can stop others from doing certain things with your copyrighted work without your permission. Of course, there are always exceptions to the rule. Exceptions include the concept of *fair use* as well as some others that we'll point out as we go along. For now, let's focus on the exclusive rights of a copyright holder:

- Reproduction
- Adaptation
- Distribution
- Performance
- Display

We go through each in a bit more detail throughout this chapter, so you can rattle them off at your next party.

Reproduction

Reproduction is straightforward. The copyright owner has the exclusive right to make copies of a copyrighted work. An exception to the exclusive right is that libraries, broadcasters, and owners of computer programs have been afforded the right to make a single copy of a copyrighted work.

Adaptation

An adaptation is a transformation of the work into another form. This could be the film version of your favorite book (as an example, for us lawyers, that would be *The Firm*) or a TV show based on a successful movie (for example, M*A*S*H). An adaptation is another name for a *derivative work*.

Some other examples of adaptations or derivative works include:

- Translations
- Musical arrangements
- Dramatizations
- Fictionalizations
- Motion picture versions
- Sound recordings
- Art reproductions
- Abridgments
- Condensations

Distribution

As the copyright owner, you have the exclusive right to sell or rent copies of the protected work (unless, of course, you provide someone else with permission to do). As you may recall, the concept of selling or renting a copyrighted work equates to *publication* of that work and can impact the duration of the term of your copyright as well as the registration procedures. The fact that distribution is an exclusive right puts a copyright owner in control of whether to publish the work. On a separate note, once you sell a copy of your work to someone else, that person now has the right to do whatever he or she wants to with that particular copy. Of course, she can't make further copies, but she can resell that single copy.

Performance

Guess what? If you write a hit song, no one is allowed to perform it publicly without your permission! The official definition of a protected performance includes reciting, rendering, playing, dancing, and acting. Therefore, playing a movie DVD without permission is prohibited. So are you breaking the law by playing the DVD you bought in your local store? Of course not! If you buy it, permission to play it is presumed. Also, you might have noticed above the words *perform publicly*. You are permitted to perform someone else's work privately, which means only for your family members and social acquaintances. Bottom line: Don't turn your living room into the local theatre.

There are also certain exceptions to the performance rule, as follows:

- Performances for charitable, religious, nonprofit, and educational purposes are okay.
- Visual arts works cannot be performed (you can't perform a painting!) so there is no exclusive performance right for visual arts works.
- Finally, and for a real twist, you are permitted to perform a sound recording (for example, play a CD)—there is no exclusive right.

However, please realize that the underlying musical composition is considered a performing arts work and performance of such a work therefore requires consent of the person who composed the music.

Objections

Remember, while playing a sound recording may not be infringement of the sound recording itself, it might be infringement of the underlying performing arts work!

Display

For all categories of copyrights other than sound recordings, the copyright owner has an exclusive right to display his or her copyrighted work. A display includes showing a copy via TV, film, or any other device or method. Once again, there are a couple of exceptions. First, if you have a legitimate copy of a copyrighted work, you're allowed to display it to viewers in its usual setting (for example, you can show off the painting you purchased in your living room to your guests). Second, others are permitted to display a copyrighted work for charitable, religious, nonprofit, and educational purposes.

Rights of Attribution and Integrity

It used to be that you could show a visual arts work (such as a painting) without crediting the creator. This led to a tremendous amount of misrepresentation (for example, "I painted the Mona Lisa"). The copyright law now provides some additional protections for folks who create a subset of visual arts works. This subset includes one-of-a-kind or limited-edition paintings, drawings, sculptures, prints, and photographs. The law prohibits people from improperly claiming they created the work. In fact, if you're the artist, you can actually claim authorship over the work even after you sell it (for example, you can tell others that you painted the beautiful picture hanging in my house). The law also says that you can't distort or mutilate a visual arts work and then attribute the new version to the creator (for example, if I paint a portrait and you distort it, you can't tell others I created the distorted portrait). Finally, as the artist, you can even prevent me from ruining the painting that you sold me. Strange, isn't it!

Stepping On Toes: Copyright Infringement

What is copyright infringement? We've just covered the exclusive rights of a copyright holder. If you own a copyrighted work, then you can stop someone from doing any of the things outlined above without your permission. However, if they don't listen to you and they actually reproduce, adapt, display, perform, or distribute your copyrighted work, then they are infringing your copyright! As you might imagine, it's not that difficult to demonstrate infringement if they are *clearly* (a) using your copyrighted work (for example, they photocopied the magazine article you wrote), and (b) doing one of the five activities exclusive to the copyright owner (such as photocopying the magazine article and handing it out on the street corner). However, in most cases of potential copyright infringement, these elements are not so clear.

Straight from the Record

Copyright infringement can be expensive! Did you know that MP3.com lost a huge copyright case in 2000 to Universal Music Group (UMG)? The court found that MP3.com willfully infringed the copyrights of thousands of UMG's compact discs with damages ranging from $118 million to $250 million. UMG and MP3.com settled prior to the final award for $53.4 million and shortly thereafter UMG bought MP3.com for $372 million.

Are They Infringing on *Your* Work?

If someone is using your exact copyrighted work (for example, the magazine article mentioned above), you don't have to worry about proving that your work was stolen. Oftentimes, however, it is less obvious whether someone used your work or a different work. Good examples can be found in the music industry. There have been many claims over the years that a musician has stolen lyrics, a background beat, a music hook, and other elements of a song and incorporated them into a different song. In these cases, courts have to decide whether it's a matter of infringement. The two key elements that can determine this are access and substantial similarity.

Access

From a logical perspective, someone who is accused of infringing a copyrighted work must have had some access to the work prior to the infringement. Suppose you've written a manuscript for a great novel but kept it locked up in a chest for the past 10 years in a Palm Beach Gardens condominium in Florida. You then discover that an individual from Vineland, New Jersey, released a novel very similar to yours. One of the things you will need to prove is that the individual had access to your chest. If not, then even an identical work would not be considered infringement. However, if a work is published or otherwise readily available, it becomes quite easy to prove access (for example, if the work is on the Internet or in a book in the library, then access is readily available).

Substantial Similarity

If you can demonstrate access to a copyrighted work, you also need to demonstrate that the work in question is *substantially similar* to your copyrighted work. Basically, if the average person concludes that the alleged infringing work incorporates important parts of your work, then this is considered substantial similarity. There are a couple of different approaches to figuring out whether there's substantial similarity between works.

Similarity of Overall Structure

It happens a lot that copyrighted works are copied, but the infringer simply tries to use different language in order to make the new work look different. In these cases, someone trying to figure out whether his or her work has been copied should look at the overall structure and how one thought flows to the next. However, to prove infringement in these situations, the structural similarities have to be pretty close (because, as we've explained, you can't protect a general idea but rather how that idea is actually expressed).

For example, if someone writes a book about a law student who gets a great job with a law firm only to uncover its fraudulent activities, the author of this book would probably not be infringing John Grisham's *The Firm*. However, if that author said the student went to Harvard Law School, got a job with a small tax firm in Memphis, Tennessee, moved there with his wife, learned that no one has ever left the firm alive, got entrapped into infidelity by the firm, uncovered connections with the mob and corresponding tax evasion by the firm and its clients, copied the relevant tax records while in the Grand Caymans at the firm's apartment and, ultimately, had to escape attempts on his life, then there's a better chance that a court would find the story a case of copyright infringement on *The Firm* (even if none of the actual dialogue from *The Firm* was used in the new book).

Straight from the Record

Courts have found that parodies of copyrighted works are permitted under certain circumstances and fall outside the exclusive rights of a copyright holder. However, this area of the law is not well established and you should consult an attorney before releasing a parody of a copyrighted work.

Partial Copying

Earlier in this chapter, we described a situation where a portion of a song is taken and used in a new song. It may have been a portion of the lyrics or a repetitive drum sequence. In these cases, the copying is fairly obvious. However, the big question is whether enough of the original work was appropriated to deem the two works substantially similar. Typically, in order to determine substantiality, you would look at the importance level of the appropriated portion in relation to the new work. If the most recognizable piece of a song (for example, the hook for "Walk this Way" by Aerosmith) is used prominently in a new song without permission, then it may be considered a case of infringement.

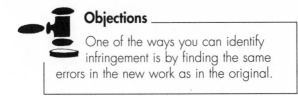

Objections

One of the ways you can identify infringement is by finding the same errors in the new work as in the original.

Licensing and Sale of Copyrights

The expression *intellectual property* contains the word *property*. As a result, you can treat intellectual property just like any other property. You can rent it (called a *license*) or sell it (called an *assignment*). You can decide under what terms you will license it (for example, you can let someone license a copyrighted work for publication in a specific magazine, and only that magazine).

Some Licensing Considerations

There are several things you may want to consider before licensing your copyrighted work to another person or a company. For purposes of this section, let's consider this example. You have painted a picture and someone (let's call this person the seller) has expressed an interest in making and selling limited-edition lithographs of your picture. You should consider the following:

- **License**. The nature of the relationship between you and the seller is that the seller is licensing the right to create a derivative work (the lithographs) and distribute it to others. You are also giving this person the

right to display the work for purposes of
increasing sales (but not, for example, to
display in an art gallery). Therefore, the
license that you provide to the seller has to
be focused (and limited) on what the seller
will be doing with the painting and the
resulting lithographs.

- **Money**. You can request some payment upfront for the right to produce the lithographs
  or you may just want to make money each
  time a lithograph is sold. Perhaps you can
  negotiate for both. Typically, this is a risk/
  reward analysis. You could probably make
  more money from sale royalties, assuming
  that the person selling the lithographs is successful. However, if you prefer safe money—
  otherwise known as *upfront money*—you'll
  probably settle for less (but at least you
  know you'll get something!).

- **Term**. For how long are you going to allow
  this person to sell your picture? If the person
  is unsuccessful, you should have the ability
  to end the relationship and either do it yourself or engage with someone who can sell
  the lithographs more successfully. As the
  copyright owner, you have a tremendous
  amount of flexibility due to your ability to
  terminate a license agreement. Many individuals have entered into a licensing arrangement only to realize later that they received
  less than they could have.

- **Geography**. Where can the seller distribute the lithographs? In your town, across the state, or across the country? Internationally? You may want to consider limiting the seller to a specific territory so that you can engage with potential sellers in other areas.

- **Limitation on number of lithographs**. So that your painting and its resulting lithographs don't become commonplace, you'll want to limit the number of lithographs that may be printed and sold.

- **Quality review**. You'll want to make sure you get a chance to review the quality of the lithographs before they are sold to ensure they meet minimum standards.

As we explained, this is just a quick list of items to consider. We do recommend consulting an attorney before you enter into a licensing arrangement.

Sale of a Copyrighted Work

You need to differentiate in your mind a sale of a copyrighted work and a sale (or assignment) of the copyright itself. In the earlier lithograph example, although the lithographs are being sold, you as the artist still have the underlying copyright in the painting. You may also decide to sell all rights to the painting *along with* the exclusive rights to reproduce, adapt, display, and distribute (we didn't mention perform, because you can't perform a visual arts work). To do this, the purchaser must have an ironclad written agreement that clearly outlines the transfer of the intellectual property rights; the physical object is not sufficient. The new copyright owner can record the transfer of ownership with the U.S. Copyright Office.

The Least You Need to Know

- The copyright owner enjoys five exclusive rights: reproduction, distribution, display, performance, and adaptation.
- Copyright infringement requires proof of access and substantial similarity.
- Just like with regular property, you can license or sell intellectual property.

Fair Use

In This Chapter

- Fair use: a permitted use of copyrighted material
- Examples of fair use
- What determines if a use is a fair use?
- What if you are not certain your use is a fair use?

All is fair in love and war. But is *all* fair in the use of copyrighted material? No. However, there are some cases that allow the use of a copyrighted work without the copyright owner's permission. These cases, which would otherwise be considered an infringement of a copyright, are referred to as *fair uses*.

What is considered fair use? There is no absolute definition for fair use. However, courts have developed a set of guidelines that help to distinguish between uses that unfairly violate the rights of the copyright owner, and uses that are reasonable, fair, customary, and expected.

In this chapter, we describe the rules of thumb that are applied in determining if a use of copyrighted material is a fair use. You will learn that some uses will almost certainly be considered as fair, and others almost certainly will not. This chapter provides guidelines to let you know when to feel secure about a use, and when you should seek the advice of an attorney.

The Rules Regarding Fair Use

The general rule is: If you want to use copyrighted material, you need to get the owner's permission. But fair use enables you to use the copyrighted material *without permission!* Why would this be allowed? Because there are certain circumstances under which it would just not be fair to prevent someone from certain uses of the copyrighted material.

The Copyright Act says that fair uses include creating copies of a copyrighted work for the purposes of criticism, comment, news reporting, teaching, scholarship, or research. In addition, the following four factors should be considered when determining if a use is a fair use:

- The purpose and character of the use
- The nature of the copyrighted work
- The amount used
- The effect of the use

There are other factors, although not included in the Copyright Act, that are considered by courts when determining if a use of copyrighted material is a fair use.

The rules of fair use are most accurately defined as guidelines that are applied in a reasonable manner on a case-by-case basis. Because there are so many different circumstances under which fair use should be considered, crafting a single rule to cover all of these situations would be an impossible task. So the courts have left us with a set of guidelines to apply against the facts of a particular case.

Application of the Fair Use Rule

The following examples are considered fair uses:

- A quotation of excerpts in a review or criticism for purposes of illustration or comment. For example, a doctor reviewing the risks of a medical procedure reported in a medical journal.

- A quotation of short passages in a scholarly or technical work for illustration or clarification of the author's observations. For example, a historian describing the evolution of literary works through the ages.

- A use in a parody of some of the content of the parodied work. A movie called *Terminated* about a robot civilization that keeps breaking down could be a parody of the movie *Terminator*.

- A summary of an address or article, with brief quotations, in a news report. For example, Fox News reporting on the contents of a political book.

- A reproduction by a library of a damaged portion of a work. For example, replacing a page that was ripped out by an unruly student.

- A reproduction by a teacher or student of a small part of a work to illustrate a lesson. For example, copying a portion of a famous speech to review in class.

- A reproduction of a work in legislative or judicial proceedings or reports. For example, including extensive passages from *Gone with the Wind* and *The Wind Done Gone* to determine if copyright infringement occurred.

- An incidental and fortuitous reproduction in a newsreel or broadcast of a work that happens to be located in the scene of the reported event. For instance, filming of a news report in front of the huge television displayed in Times Square may result in copyrighted material (that is, a movie or show) being included in the report.

Four Factors for Determining Fair Use

What do you need to do if your use does not align with one of these examples? First, you should compare your use against the following four factors. In some situations, you will feel quite comfortable that your use is a fair use. In other scenarios, you will be quite certain that your use is not a fair use. And then there is the fuzzy zone where you are still not certain.

Each of the four factors raises several questions. Depending on how you answer each question will help to determine whether your use is a fair use, an infringing use, or in the fuzzy zone. You can think of it as a two-sided scale of justice—on one side is the fair use and on the other, the infringing use. When the scale is balanced, you are in the fuzzy zone. As the fair use side gets weighed down, you move from the fuzzy zone into fair use. As the infringing use side gets closer to the ground, you move from the fuzzy zone into infringing use. So let's get started.

Factor 1—The Purpose and Character of the Use

In determining whether a use is a fair use, the courts will look at the purpose and characteristics of your use. A quick test is to check whether the use is for nonprofit purposes (this leans toward fair use) or for commercial reasons (this leans toward an infringing use). However, this test by itself is not enough to make a determination.

- **Is your use a nonprofit use?** If the answer is yes, put a jelly bean on the fair use side of the scale. What is a nonprofit use? Simply put, it is a use that is not intended to generate revenue or commercial gain for the user. The next seven questions will help you determine if your use is a nonprofit use.

- **Is your use for educational purposes?** If the answer is yes, put a jelly bean on the fair use side of the scale. Educational purposes can include many uses, such as in the case of a teacher making copies of an article to be distributed to the students as a learning aid for one particular lesson or a student making copies of a reference to study and mark up while preparing a research paper.

- **Is your use for personal purposes?** If the answer is yes, put a jelly bean on the fair use side of the scale. Personal uses can be a little tricky though. It is not a free ticket to use someone's copyrighted material. A few examples of personal uses that are fair use include:

  - Video taping a television program to watch at a later time

  - Making a back-up copy of your software disks

  - Copying a song from one medium, such as a compact disk, to another medium, such as a computer hard disk drive, for personal use

- **Is your use for the purposes of criticism?** If the answer is yes, put a jelly bean on the fair use side of the scale. If you copy excerpts from a copyrighted work and use them as illustrative examples for the purpose of criticism, it is a fair use. Typical examples of this type of use include:

  - A scholar criticizing a theory proposed by another scholar

- Copying portions of a particular singer's songs to illustrate that the singer has strong political views.

- **Is your use for the purposes of commentary?** If the answer is yes, put a jelly bean on the fair use side of the scale. The commentary can't simply be a recitation of large portions of the work with supporting comments. A commentary for the purposes of fair use must include only limited excerpts from the work being commented on, typically just the minimum amount necessary to make the point.

- **Is your use for the purpose of reporting news?** If the answer is yes, put a jelly bean on the fair use side of the scale.

- **Is your use for the parody purposes?** If the answer is yes, put a jelly bean on the fair use side of the scale. For more information on what defines a parody, see the "Parody" section later in this chapter.

- **Is your use a transformative use?** If the answer is yes, put a jelly bean on the fair use side of the scale. Transformative use might sound really complicated, but it is really not so difficult to understand. If you are using an existing work and augmenting it with new and creative efforts, then you are likely transforming the work or performing a transformative use of it. However, if you are simply duplicating the copyrighted work, the copy is not a result of transformative use.

- **Is your use a commercial use?** If the answer is yes, put a jelly bean on the infringing side of the scale. A commercial use is one that is intended to generate profit for the user. This profit could include money as well as fame, recognition, advertising, or the like. A few additional questions will help you determine if your use is a commercial use. You will need to put an additional jelly bean on the infringing use side of the scale for each "yes" to the following questions.

  - Will you sell copies of the new work that includes the copyrighted material?

  - Will your new work be used to entertain others?

  - If your use is through an entertainment broadcast, will you receive financial benefit for the broadcast through advertising or payment?

  - Will the new work you create fail to recognize the original author?

Go ahead and give yourself one jelly bean for getting through those questions. You are going to need a few more though, as we move through the next three factors.

Factor 2—The Nature of the Copyrighted Work

The courts will also look at the nature of the copyrighted work when making a determination of fair use. Sometimes, the work is naturally intended to be copied for certain purposes. A perfect example would be a crossword puzzle in a newspaper. If you are getting ready to go on an extended business trip, you may save up a few newspapers and photocopy some crossword puzzles to take with you.

The copyrighted work can include a collection of well-known or easily discovered facts that are put together into a work without adding any imagination or creativity. For example, the four factors presented in this chapter are well-known facts that are not copyrighted. However, considerable imaginative effort is being put forth in making this chapter interesting to read rather than just reciting the facts. You are free to copy the four factors but you cannot copy the manner in which we present the four facts in this chapter.

Also, when an author publishes a work, he or she should anticipate that others will have access to the work. However, if the author does not publish a work but keeps it for personal use instead, then he or she would not expect others to be using the work. Thus, for unpublished copyrighted works, it is more difficult to justify a fair use.

Here are a few questions you need to answer regarding the nature of the copyrighted work that you plan to use.

- **Is the copyrighted work primarily factual?** If the answer is yes, put a jelly bean on the fair use side of the scale.

- **Is the copyrighted work primarily historical?** If the answer is yes, put a jelly bean on the fair use side of the scale.

- **If the copyrighted work is primarily factual, are the facts easily obtained by doing simple research?** If the answer is yes, put a jelly bean on the fair use side of the scale.

- **If the copyrighted work is primarily factual, does it appear that the authors had to engage in extensive research to derive the factual content?** If the answer is yes, put a jelly bean on the infringing use side of the scale.

- **Did the authors of the copyrighted work appear to use creativity in creating the work?** If the answer is yes, put a jelly bean on the infringing use side of the scale.

- **Is the copyrighted work fictional?** If the answer is yes, put a jelly bean on the infringing use side of the scale.

- **Is the copyrighted work published?** If the answer is yes, put a jelly bean on the fair use side of the scale.

- **Is the copyrighted work unpublished?** If the answer is yes, put a jelly bean on the infringing use side of the scale.

Factor 3—The Amount of Copyright Information Used

The Copyright Act focuses on "the amount and substantiality of the portion used in relation to the copyrighted work as a whole." The simple test is to

establish the amount of the copyrighted work that
was used. However, this is not the only aspect of
the test. Another element to take into account is
the "substantiality of the portion." This means that
even if you copy a small amount of a small copyright work, it could be a substantial portion of the
copyrighted work. For example, copying 300 words
of a 600-word document is a substantial portion.
However, copying 300 words of a 1000-page book
may not be considered a substantial portion.

Here are a few questions regarding the amount of
the copyrighted work that you plan to use.

- **Are you using a small amount of the
  work?** If the answer is yes, put a jelly bean
  on the fair use side of the scale.

- **Are you using a small percentage of the
  work?** If the answer is yes, put a jelly bean
  on the fair use side of the scale.

- **Are you using the minimal amount of the
  work necessary to achieve your goal,
  such as in a criticism or a commentary of
  the work?** If the answer is yes, put a jelly
  bean on the fair use side of the scale.

- **Does your use incorporate an incidental
  or unimportant portion of the work?** If
  the answer is yes, put a jelly bean on the fair
  use side of the scale.

- **Does your use incorporate the essence of
  the work?** If the answer is yes, put a jelly
  bean on the infringing use side of the scale.

- **Are you using a large amount of the work?** If the answer is yes, put a jelly bean on the infringing use side of the scale.

- **Are you including portions of the work that are not necessary in achieving your goal, such as in a criticism or a commentary of the work?** If the answer is yes, put a jelly bean on the infringing use side of the scale.

- **Are you using a large percentage of the work or the whole work?** If the answer is yes, put a jelly bean on the infringing use side of the scale.

Factor 4—The Effect of the Use

The Copyright Act focuses on "the effect of the use upon the potential market for or value of the copyrighted work." This factor must be viewed a little differently than the other three factors. The reason for this: If the use is weighing heavily on the fair use side, then the effect on the potential market becomes irrelevant.

Before looking at this factor, you should make sure that you have analyzed your use in light of the first three factors. If you determine that your use is a fair use, then you can ignore this factor. However, if you determine that your use is not a fair use or that it falls in or near the fuzzy zone, then you should consider this fourth factor with very much care.

Okay, so let's go through the last set of questions. Hopefully you haven't run out of jelly beans yet!

- **Do you own a legitimate copy of the original copyrighted work upon which your new work is based?** If the answer is yes, put a jelly bean on the fair use side of the scale.

- **Will your use have a negative impact on the sales of the original copyrighted work (such as, reducing sales)?** If the answer is yes, put a jelly bean on the infringing use side of the scale.

- **Is the original work still in print or available for purchase?** If the answer is yes, put a jelly bean on the infringing use side of the scale.

- **Has the copyright owner obtained royalties through licensing the copyrighted work?** If the answer is yes, put a jelly bean on the infringing use side of the scale.

- **Are you going to be marketing the new work in a similar fashion as the original work (for example, selling it in book store)?** If the answer is yes, put a jelly bean on the infringing use side of the scale.

- **Would others be likely to purchase your new work instead of the original work?** If the answer is yes, put a jelly bean on the infringing use side of the scale.

- **Will your use result in distributing a large number of copies of the new work?** If the answer is yes, put a jelly bean on the infringing use side of the scale.

- **Are you able to identify the copyright owner of the copyrighted work?** If the answer is yes, put a jelly bean on the infringing use side of the scale.

Parody

Creating a parody of a copyrighted work is an interesting situation. Basically, a parody is a new work that is based on another work and makes fun of that other work or its author.

Parody is a form of criticism that can result in casting the original work's author in an unfavorable light. So you can imagine that the author may be quite reluctant in granting permission to the person wanting to create the parody. However, fair use allows for creation of parodies.

If you are planning on creating a parody, you should be careful. The lines between parody and copyright infringement can be very blurry. For example, suppose you want to create a parody of a song by changing the lyrics but still using the original music. The song actually has at least two forms of copyright protection—the lyrics and the music. So simply changing the lyrics may not be enough to get fair use. However, it may—the Supreme Court has ruled that 2 Live Crew's rendition of Roy Orbinson's "Pretty Woman" was a parody.

Are You Certain Your Use Is a Fair Use?

If you find yourself in the fuzzy zone or the infringing use zone, you have at least four options to consider.

One option is just to plow ahead and hope for the best. We don't really recommend this option. Infringement of copyrights can be very costly and, in some circumstances, may even result in spending some time behind bars.

Another option is to seek the advice of an attorney. An attorney can review your use and prepare a *legal opinion* concerning your use. A legal opinion is a written document prepared by an attorney that describes your use of copyright material and the attorney's prediction of how a court will interpret your use in view of the law.

Another option is simply to ask the copyright owner for permission. This is called getting a license. The copyright owner may be happy and thrilled that someone is recognizing his or her work and grant you permission. The permission may come as a free gift or the copyright owner may require some sort of compensation for the use. There are no rules as to how much it costs to obtain a license—it is negotiated.

Another option, in contrast to the NIKE slogan, is *just don't do it*. If you are not certain whether your use is a fair use, and you don't have the copyright owner's permission, you might want to consider an alternative solution.

The Least You Need to Know

- You can use a copyrighted work without permission if your use qualifies as a fair use.

- There are four factors to consider when determining whether your use is a fair use but there is no hard-and-fast rule that guarantees you this safety.

- If you are uncertain whether your use is a fair use, you should seek counsel from an attorney to determine if you are headed for legal trouble.

- Don't forget that you can always ask the author or copyright owner for permission.

Chapter 5

Obtaining Copyright Protection

In This Chapter

- Automatic copyright protection
- Filling out forms and registering your copyright
- To use or not to use a copyright attorney

We've discussed many of the reasons why copyrights are an important way to protect your writings and other works. But how do you go about the process of obtaining a copyright? In the world of intellectual property protection, a copyright is actually a very easy form of protection to obtain.

In this chapter, we describe what you need to know to secure your rights and maximize your protection. We also help you to make sure you're protected beyond the borders of the United States.

Automatic Protection

Few things in life are free. And almost none are free, automatic, and potentially valuable. Surprisingly, one of those things is a copyright. As we write each of the words in this book, copyright protection automatically attaches to the language and the unique way in which we arrange our words. Therefore, registration is not required.

Now you're saying: "Why have I been wasting all my time reading this book if I get copyright protection automatically!" You haven't wasted your time at all. There are significant benefits to registering your copyright with the U.S. Copyright Office.

Straight from the Record

One of the most famous copyrights is the original disc operating system that controls personal computers. In 1981, Microsoft acquired the copyright from Seattle Computer Products for $50,000, renamed it MS-DOS and licensed it to IBM. Microsoft has so far created a $300 billion empire on the foundation of MS-DOS.

Benefits of Federal Registration

You may ask why you'd need to bother registering your copyright if you are automatically protected. As we mentioned above, copyright registration makes a public record of general information related to a copyright. Registration gives other people notice that you have and claim a copyright and provides the following benefits:

- Before you can file an infringement suit related to a work created in the United States, you must register your copyright.

- Your registration of a work within five years of its publication will establish the validity of your copyright and the facts stated in the copyright certificate in court.

- Your registration of a work within three months of publication or prior to an infringement of the work will allow you to seek a set range of damages (called *statutory damages*) and attorney's fees in an infringement action rather than having to prove how much damage someone's infringement caused you (which is often difficult to prove). Statutory damages typically range from $500 to $20,000 per violation and sometimes even go up to $100,000 per violation. Otherwise, the copyright owner can only receive an award of actual damages and profits. Typically, it's either too difficult to prove the actual damage caused by a copyright infringement, or the amount is too small to make it worth suing.

- Your registration enables you to obtain additional protection from the U.S. Customs Service against the importation of infringing copies of your copyrighted work.

Federal "Do-It-Yourself" Copyright Filing

You can either pay a lawyer a few hundred dollars to register your work or you can do it yourself after paying the very reasonable price of this book. That's not to say that utilizing a lawyer for registration doesn't have its advantages. However, step-by-step, we'll go through the process for filing your U.S. registration.

Step 1: Throw It in a Bucket!

Depending on the kind of work you created, you will be required to fill out a special registration form. Therefore, it's critical that you figure out which category your work falls into. Refer back to Chapter 2 to figure out what type of work you want to protect, from the following list:

- Literary works
- Visual arts works
- Performing arts works
- Sound recordings
- Serials and periodicals

How to Fill Out the Registration Form

Each of the above categories of copyrightable works has its own registration form. Many parts of these forms require similar information, but a few have specific twists. That is why it's so important to categorize your work properly.

The registration forms can be obtained from the U.S. Copyright Office website at www.copyright.gov, under the section entitled "How to Register a Work." You may also get forms from the Copyright Office in person, by mailing in a request, or by calling their 24-hour forms hotline at 202-707-9100.

The Registration Form: Short vs. Long (vs. Group)

Some of the copyright categories have one form while others have two: a short form and a long form. For serials and periodicals, there is also a group form. We explain which categories have different forms and how to choose the right form.

- **Sound recordings and visual arts.** If your work falls into either of these categories, guess what? You're in luck. There is only one form to fill out.

- **Literary works or performing arts works.** You have a choice between a short form and a long form. You will choose the short form if *all* of the following apply:

  - You are the only author and copyright owner of the work, *and*

  - The work was not a *work made for hire* (see Chapter 6 for a detailed description of what this means—don't assume you understand it), *and*

  - The work is completely new (which means it does not contain a *substantial* amount of material that has been previously published or registered or is in the public domain), *and*

- For performing arts works *only* (if your work is literary *and* you meet the requirements for the last three bullet points, use the short form), the work is not a motion picture or other audiovisual work.

- **Serials and periodicals.** You have a choice between a short form and a long form. You will choose the short form if *all* of the following apply:
  - The work is part of a collective work (meaning a collection of separate pieces, like a magazine), *and*
  - The majority of the work is new, *and*
  - The author is a citizen or a resident of the United States, *and*
  - The work is a work made for hire, *and*
  - The author and person (or business) claiming ownership of the copyright are the same; *and*
  - The work was first published (see the explanation under Creation and Publication below) in the United States

There is also a group form that is sometimes used for a serial or periodical. We're not going to spend much time on this form because it is not used very often. This type of form is typically used only for a serial publication that is published no more than once a week and all issues are published within a three-month period! If you believe you fall into this category, we highly recommend visiting www. copyright.gov and clicking on "Serials and Periodicals." This link will explain the mechanics of the group form for serials and periodicals.

The Registration Form: General Information

While there are different registration forms depending on the category of work you submit, the registration forms are extremely similar.

Long Registration Forms

The long registration forms have nine spaces that need to be completed, as explained in the following sections.

Space 1: Title

You must give your copyrighted work a title for identification purposes. If the actual work you are submitting already has a title (for example, *The Pocket Idiot's Guide to Copyrights*), then copy that title *completely and exactly* (their words, not ours). Your attention to detail here will help you locate your registration later, if you should misplace the registration number.

You can also list previous or alternative titles. This provides you with an opportunity to give the work an alternative title so if you or someone else is searching for it later, it can be found under more than one title. For example, a song like the Beatles "She Loves You" could be titled "She Loves You" as well as "Yeah, Yeah, Yeah."

For literary works or visual arts works, you must also indicate whether the work you are submitting is a contribution to a serial, a periodical, or a collection of works (and you must list the related work). For performing arts works, you must indicate the general nature or character of the work you are submitting (for example, musical play, drama, song lyrics, and so on).

Space 2: Author(s)

You must provide the name of the author, or authors (if more than one) of the work. Unless the work is a work made for hire (see Chapter 6), the author is the person or persons who created the work and you have to list each person's full legal name. If the work is a work made for hire, then the author is the person or company who hired or employed the creator of the work. Dates of birth (and death, if applicable) of the author are also required in this section.

In addition, the "nature of authorship" must be described in this section. For visual arts works, a variety of choices is provided. However, for other types of works, you are required to briefly describe your authorship. The Copyright Office doesn't want you to explain the work you are submitting in this section; they just want to know how you contributed to it. Typical answers for this section might include: "entire text" or "editorial revision, plus additional new material" for literary works, "music only" or "music and lyrics" for sound recordings, and "compilation and English translation" for performing arts works. For serials and periodicals, you must also select "collective work," in the event an organization directed, controlled, or supervised the creation of the work as a whole.

Space 3: Creation and Publication

The creation date and publication date may not be the same. The creation date is the date that the work was recorded on a physical medium (see Chapter 1). A good example is a song that was made up and recorded at the same time. If you created the work over a period of time, you would put the date when you completed the entire work you are submitting. For example, the date of this book's creation would be the date of its completion, rather than the date we wrote our first word.

The publication date is the date the work was first distributed for sale, lease, rental, or other transfer. Therefore, the publication date for this book would be the date it was first distributed to bookstores and others for sale.

Space 4: Claimant(s)

The claimant is the person, or company, who owns the copyrighted work. Oftentimes, the author and the claimant are the same. Other times, an author might sell the copyright to someone else (for example, a photographer takes a picture and then sells it to a tabloid newspaper). If you have a situation in which the author sold the copyright to someone else, you must include a brief statement describing how the transfer occurred (for example, *by written contract* or *by will*).

Space 5: Previous Registration

This section of the registration form is designed to determine whether the work you are submitting is based on another copyrighted work (for example, the movie version of a book). Your answers to these questions will help the Copyright Office determine whether any basis for a new registration exists. Remember, it's okay to seek registration for a work that has been changed in a significant way from its prior version. However, as common sense would dictate, only one registration can apply to a specific work.

Space 6: Derivative Work or Compilation

You only need to complete this section if the work you are submitting is a changed version (a substantially different version of a previously registered work), a compilation, or a derivative work (go back to Chapter 2 to read about these items).

Spaces 7, 8, and 9: Fee, Correspondence, Certification, and Return Address

These spaces are purely administrative. Simply fill in the required information.

Short Registration Forms

The short registration forms for literary works, performing arts works, or serials and periodicals are easier versions of the long forms. If you meet the requirements explained above, you have to provide the information on only one page of the short registration form.

The short forms for literary works and performing arts works have all of the same sections as the long forms, but many of the questions from the long forms have been eliminated. Bottom line: It's short and simple!

For serials and periodicals, the Copyright Office has quickened the repeated filings that copyright owners must do routinely (every time a new work in the series is published). The short form contains only three primary sections—title, name and address, and date of publication. Once again, it's a much simpler form than the long one.

Filing Procedures

Now that you have completed the correct forms, you are ready to file your copyright registration. There are some particulars you will need to know about filing your registration.

You need to include these items in your correspondence:

- **Cover letter.** Your cover letter should explain the contents of what you are sending and request the Copyright Office's registration of your work.
- **The completed registration form.** You should fill out all appropriate sections as described above.
- **Money.** As you might expect, filing isn't free. Generally, each copyright registration

requires a payment of $30. There are certain additional fees for group serials and periodicals ($10 per issue, with a minimum of $30) and group registration of newspapers ($55). The check should be made payable to "Register of Copyrights." Make sure you indicate the title of your registration on the memo line of the check.

- **Submission of the work**. Depending on the form of the work, you will need to submit either the entire work or a sample of the work to be registered; it is called a deposit. Please note that, unlike a bank, the Copyright Office will *not* return your deposit, so make sure you don't provide them with your only copy! Below, we've listed the typical deposit requirements. If you don't feel your work falls into one of the deposit requirements, it may fall into a special deposit class. If that's the case, call the U.S. Copyright Office at 202-707-9100 and ask them about your specific situation. Otherwise, here's how it typically works:

  - If the work was first published in the United States on or after January 1, 1978, you must submit two complete copies of your best edition.

  - If the work was first published in the United States before January 1, 1978, you must submit two complete copies of the work as first published.

- If the work was first published outside the United States, you must send one complete copy of the work as first published.

- If the work is a computer program, you must print out and submit one clear copy in source code of the first 25 and the last 25 pages of the program (or all of it, if it's 50 pages or less).

The mailing address for copyright submissions is:

> Library of Congress
> Copyright Office
> 101 Independence Avenue, S.E.
> Washington, D.C. 20559-6000

The best way to send your registration to the Copyright Office is by Express Mail (offered through the United States Post Office) or another nationally recognized delivery system. Make sure your mailing is return receipt requested or confirmed delivery because you will want to make sure the Copyright Office actually received your package.

Make a Copy!

Mailed items are often lost at the U.S. Copyright Office. In fact, due to new mail handling requirements at government facilities (due to the Anthrax incidents in 2001 and 2002), all mail is screened at an outside facility before it is delivered to the Copyright Office. As a result, receipt of your mail can be delayed three to five days. Because of these issues, it is imperative that you make a copy of *everything* you send to them. If you have not received any correspondence from the U.S. Copyright Office within six months of your mailing, you should contact them to determine whether they lost your filing.

Make sure you create a file in your house where you keep all of the copies mentioned above, together with your Express Mail receipt. When you receive correspondence from the Copyright Office, make sure you put it in this file.

> ### Straight from the Record
>
> Section 407 of the Copyright Act requires *mandatory* deposit of all works within three months of their publication in the United States (this differs from registration).

What You'll Get Back from the Copyright Office

Once you have filed your registration, the waiting begins. Your copyright registration becomes effective on the day the Copyright Office receives your mailing, assuming that your application is in order (it is good to use a confirmed delivery method so you can prove when they should have received your registration). Typically, you will receive your official notice of registration within four to five months of your mailing date. In the event you have made an error in your application, you will likely be able to correct that error and your registration will be retro-active to your original filing date (they will send you correspondence indicating the error and how to amend your registration to correct it).

Using the "Circle C" ©

The "circle c" otherwise known as © puts the world on notice that you claim a copyright in the work it is attached to. The proper way to use the © is in connection with the year of first publication (you wouldn't need to put the "circle c" if no one else will see your work!) and the copyright owner's name, as follows: © 2003 John Doe. You are permitted to re-place the symbol © with the word "copyright." Many others combine these concepts as follows: "© Copy-right 2004 John Doe." In reality, the use of the sym-bol is not even required, which is why there's so much flexibility in its positioning. Use of the notice does not require permission from, or registration with, the Copyright Office.

The Least You Need to Know

- Copyright protection automatically attaches to your work.
- There are significant benefits to federally registering your copyright.
- An attorney can be very helpful in the copy-right process.

Chapter 6

The Life of a Copyright

In This Chapter

- Historical evolution of copyright protection
- The duration of protection for newer and older works
- The effect of providing copyright notice
- The expiration of copyright protection

An author's ownership in his or her work begins at the very moment the work is created. For example, as soon as a poet writes a poem, he or she creates a copyright ownership in that poem. But when does the author's ownership end? This chapter focuses on how long the author or creator of a work has copyright protection for that work (that is, the duration of time that the author can prevent others from copying the work).

Determining how long copyright protection will endure for a particular work is not as complicated as multivariable calculus, but it can still be quite confusing. The duration of copyright protection for a particular work depends on several factors including:

- When the work was created;
- Who the creator was;
- Whether the work was published;
- The characteristics of the work; and
- Whether the authors are still living.

It is somewhat simple to determine the duration of copyright protection for recently or soon to be created works. We address the duration of copyright protection for these works first. Determining the duration of protection for works that have been created prior to January 1, 1978, is a more complicated task.

The Historical Evolution

Experts claim that the first formal copyright protection can be traced to the Statute of Anne, which was passed by the English Parliament in 1710. The duration of protection for a copyrighted work in the Statute of Anne was 14 years.

In the New World where everything is twice as good as in the Old World, the United States Congress passed a new copyright law that established a term of protection of 28 years under the U.S. Act of 1790.

Not to be outdone by the early founders of our nation, the duration of copyright protection was once again changed under the 1909 Copyright Act, which was amended again in 1947 by adding an additional renewable term of 28 years to the initial 28-year term, resulting in the total of 56 years.

In the last 40 years alone, the laws regarding the duration of a copyright have changed 11 times. A monumental change occurred in the 1976 Copyright Act when the duration of protection for copyrighted works created on or after January 1, 1978, was extended to the life of the author plus 50 years. For works created before January 1, 1978, the 1976 Copyright Act provided an additional 19-year extension.

Another recent change occurred in 1998 upon the signing of the Sonny Bono Copyright Term Extension Act. Under certain circumstances, the Sonny Bono Copyright Term Extension Act extends the copyright duration an additional 20 years. The good news for copyright holders is that the longer the term is extended, the more the copyright holder can benefit from the work. The bad news is that if the trend continues, this chapter will need to be updated in the near future.

Straight from the Record

Do you know what the relationship is between Sonny Bono and Mickey Mouse? Well, if it wasn't for the Sonny Bono Copyright Term Extension Act, the copyright protection for the beloved Mickey Mouse character would have expired in the year 2003.

There are two main concerns regarding the duration of copyright protection. The first concern is for the authors or owners who are primarily interested in how long their works will be protected. The second concern is for the public that wants to use the work without infringing the copyright. These individuals are interested in the date that the copyrighted work will pass into the *public domain*.

Public Domain

What does it mean for a work to be *in the public domain*? All works that are not protected under copyright laws are in the public domain. If a work is in the public domain and not subject to other forms of protection, it can be freely copied or used. However, prior to using a work that is assumed to be in the public domain, a person or company should obtain proof that the work is indeed in the public domain and that it is not covered by any other means of legal protection such as trademark protection, patent protection, moral rights, and so on.

Newer Works

The Copyright Act of 1976 identified a magical date for the duration of copyright protection. The magical date is January 1, 1978. Works created on or after this magical date fall into the newer works category for determining the duration of copyright protection. The duration of copyright protection for these works follows one of two rules:

- The life plus 70 years rule
- The 95/120 years rule

The Life Plus 70 Years Rule

For works that were created on or after January 1, 1978, the duration of the copyright protection is the life of the author plus 70 years. Once the work is created, the duration of protection begins. Upon the death of the author, the duration of the protection is fixed to expire in 70 years.

If more than one author created the work, the life plus 70 years rule still applies. However, the final 70 years of the copyright protection do not begin until the last surviving author is deceased.

The 95/120 Years Rule

The 95/120 years rule applies when the life of the author cannot be determined (for example, pseudonymous and anonymous works). A pseudonymous work is when the author hides behind a pen name to protect his or her identity. Under the 95/120 years rule, the duration of copyright protection is either 95 years from the first publication of the work or 120 years from the creation of the work—whichever is shorter.

Under the 95/120 years rule, the shortest duration for copyright protection is 95 years and occurs when the work is created and published at the same time. The maximum duration for copyright protection is 120 years and occurs when the work is created but not published for at least 25 years after the creation.

For example, if a work is created in the year 2000 and never published, the copyright protection will end in the year 2120. If the work is published in the year 2030, the copyright protection will still end in the year 2120 rather than the year 2125 (95 years from the publication date) because 120 years is the maximum duration.

The 95/120 years rule is also applied to *works made for hire*. An example of a work made for hire is when a company hires one or more individuals to create a work on behalf of a company. The individuals hired to create the work are not the copyright owners of the work even though they are the creators. The company owns the copyright. Because the life of a company can vary greatly (that is, from instant death to perpetual life), it does not make sense to tie the duration of protection to life. Instead, the 95/120 years rule applies for works made for hire.

Straight from the Record

Samuel Langhorne Clemens wrote several books under the pen name of Mark Twain. "Mark Twain" was a phrase that boatmen used to indicate two fathoms of water (or 12 feet), the depth needed for a boat's safe passage along the river. Even though it is a well-known fact that Samuel Langhorne Clemens was Mark Twain, the 95/120 years rule would apply to the duration of copyright protection if the pseudonymous works were not registered under the author name of Mr. Clemens.

Older Works

Works published before 1923 or created before 1978 fall into the older works category.

Works Published Before 1923

Any works published prior to 1923 entered the public domain on January 1, 1998. What about the situation where a work is created but not published? For example, on a boring rainy day you are rummaging around in your grandparents' attic and you come across a dusty old diary. Upon reading the diary, you discover it was written by your great grandfather who was a newspaper reporter during World War I. After he returned to the United States, your great grandfather wrote a memoir in this diary. No one ever published the diary. Is this diary considered to be in the public domain? We answer the question later in this chapter.

Proper Pointers _____

What is a *published* work? Publishing occurs when copies of a work are distributed to the public through a sale or other transfer of ownership such as renting, leasing, or lending. Simply displaying or performing a work in public does not constitute a publication of the work.

Works Created Before 1978

The duration of copyright protection for works that have roots before the magical date of January 1, 1978, mainly relies on four factors:

- When the work was created.
- When the work was published or registered.
- Whether or not a copyright notice was included.
- Whether the copyright was renewed.

Created but Never Published or Registered

If a work was created before January 1, 1978, but was not published or registered, the duration of copyright protection is determined by the life of the author plus 70 years or 95/120 years, according to rules we've outlined in the previous section.

Let's revisit the example of the old diary found in the attic. As you recall, the diary was written but never published. We did not indicate whether the diary was in the public domain. Well, here is the answer. Suppose that the diary was written in 1914. In this situation, we have a work created prior to 1923 but never published. Thus, the duration of protection is determined by the life of the author plus 70 years. Suppose your great grandfather was 20 years old when he wrote his diary and he passed away in 1985. Upon his death, the duration of copyright protection for the diary will extend for an additional 70 years. In this example, the diary is not in the public domain and the copyright protection will extend through the year 2060.

Straight from the Record

On what day does copyright protection end? According to Section 305 of Title 17 of the United States Code, the duration of copyright protection runs to the end of the calendar year in which the copyright protection expires.

Published or Registered Between 12/31/23 and 1/1/78

If a work was published or registered after December 31, 1923, but before January 1, 1978, then an initial term of duration for the copyright protection is 28 years from the date the work was registered. In other words, the initial term of protection will expire 28 years from publishing or registering the work unless the registration is renewed.

As you recall, for works created before 1978 but not published, the life plus 70 years rule applies. Suppose a work created prior to January 1, 1978, is published between January 1, 1978, and December 31, 2002? There is a special rule for this situation; it states that the copyright protection will not expire prior to December 31, 2047.

Straight from the Record

For composite works (or works based on other copyrighted material), the duration of copyright protection for the entire work is based on the creation and publication of the composite work, not its components.

Renewable Terms

Prior to the expiration of the initial 28-year term, the copyright protection can be renewed. The length of the renewal period is based on when the initial term expires.

If the initial 28-year term for copyright protection was still active on January 1, 1978, then the term can be renewed for an additional 67 years from the expiration of the initial 28-year term.

If the initial 28-year term or a renewal term for copyright protection is still active as of the effective date of the Sonny Bono Copyright Term Extension Act—October 27, 1998—the total duration of copyright protection is 95 years from the publishing date of the work.

Renewing the Copyright Protection

A copyright is renewed by filing the proper documentation and the required fees with the Copyright Office. The copyright must be renewed during the last year of the initial 28-year term of copyright protection.

Initially, the renewable term was 28 years. However, the 1976 Copyright Act extended this term by 19 years and the Sonny Bono Copyright Term Extension Act extended the renewable term an additional 20 years. Thus, the renewable term is now 67 years.

The 67-year renewable term is available if the work was published or registered after the author's death but before January 1, 1978.

Let's look at the old diary example again. Suppose that copies of the diary had been sold in 1923 and the copyright was registered. Is the diary in the public domain? The initial term of copyright protection was 28 years or through the end of 1951. The duration of protection in the renewal terms would extend through the year 2018—67 years.

Copyright Notice

In 1988, the United States adopted the Berne Convention Implementation Act of 1988. Prior to the adoption of this act, the duration of copyright protection could be drastically affected if the work was published without a proper copyright notice. Any work without a copyright notice published prior to March 1, 1989, was deemed to be in the public domain.

Today, the inclusion of copyright notice is not necessary but it is strongly recommended.

Expiration or Termination of a Copyright

What happens to a work at the expiration or termination of copyright protection? At this point, the work becomes a *public work*. However, the expiration of copyright protection does not necessarily mean that the work can be freely copied or distributed. The work may be protected under other laws such as trademarks, patents, moral rights, or other legal forms of protection.

Application of the Duration Rules

We have now laid out the various rules that determine the duration of copyright protection. The following table provides an overview of how these rules are applied.

Copyright Life Summary Table

Event	Protection Duration	Status
Created on or after January 1, 1978	Life plus 70 years or 95/120 years rules apply	Will enter the public domain in accordance with the life plus 70 years or 95/120 years rules

Event	Protection Duration	Status
Status of author unknown	95/120 years rule applies	Will enter or has entered the public domain the earlier of 95 years from publication or 120 years from creation
Author becomes known for anonymous work	Life plus 70 years rule applies	Will enter or has entered the public domain 70 years from author's death
Published before 1923	Initial term of 28 years Renewed term of 47 years	Entered public domain on or before January 1, 1998
Created before 1923 but not published	Life plus 70 years or 95/120 years rules apply	Entered public domain after December 31, 2002 if author deceased before 1932 or, for the 95/120 years rule, if the work was created on or before 1882
Published on or after January 1, 1923 but before January 1, 1978	Initial term of 28 years Renewed term of 67 years	Will enter public domain 95 years from publication date if properly renewed

continues

Copyright Life Summary Table   (continued)

Event	Protection Duration	Status
Created before January 1, 1923, and published on or after January 1, 1978, but before December 31, 2002	Life plus 70 years or 95/120 years rules apply	Will enter public domain on January 1, 2048, if author deceased before 1978 or, for the 95/120 years rule, if the work was created on or before 1927

The Least You Need to Know

- Unless the law changes again, copyright protection for a work will eventually end.
- To determine the duration of copyright protection, find out who the authors were, the date of creation and the date of publication, then apply the appropriate rules.
- Before using any work, you should determine if the copyright protection is still active.

Chapter 7

Do You Own a Copyright?

In This Chapter

- Copyright ownership basics
- Employer/employee copyright issues
- Losing your ownership in a copyright
- Gaining ownership in a copyright

Betcha didn't know that you are the owner of a copyright! But most certainly you are. Think back to that glorious day in kindergarten when your teacher made you wear a smock to protect your clothes, put a fresh clean piece of construction paper on an easel, and let you grab a handful of finger paint out of the jar. The moment you started rubbing that finger paint onto the canvas, you began creating a work of art fit for attaching to your mother's refrigerator with those little fruit magnets. Believe it or not, that finger painting is a piece of art that can be protected through copyright law. And guess who owns the copyright? That's right, you do!

In this chapter, we describe the how and when of the creation of copyright protection. You will learn that creating copyrighted works is very simple. Most people have created hundreds, if not thousands of items that can be protected under copyright laws.

You may create a work that can be protected by copyrights but someone else may own the copyright. By reading this chapter, you will learn to determine when you are the copyright owner and when someone else holds the copyright of the work that you have created.

You will also learn how you can lose your copyright ownership, or how you can knowingly or unknowingly give the ownership to someone else.

Copyright Creators as Owners

What are the requirements for owning a copyright? As we already mentioned, they are actually pretty simple. In fact, there are just four requirements:

- It has to fall into a copyright type category.
- It has to be original.
- It has to be in a physical form.
- You have to be the author.

Therefore, as a copyright creator (or author), you will be considered the copyright owner unless you knowingly or unknowingly transfer it to someone else.

The concept of authorship of a copyright can be difficult, so you may want to pay special attention here.

Are You the Author?

The author of a work is the owner of the copyright. In general, the author of a work is the person who originates or creates the work. Going back to your kindergarten finger painting example—you smeared the finger paint on the canvas—you are the author and you own the copyright.

Suppose you are dictating a chapter of your latest novel to your assistant and he or she feverishly captures your every word. Is the assistant the author? Your assistant certainly was instrumental in putting the chapter into a tangible medium, but you created the story and you are the author. Your assistant merely recorded your ideas onto a tangible medium. This does not qualify as authorship.

Suppose Preacher Smith is delivering an eloquent sermon and you are feverishly taking notes—undoubtedly so that you can remind your spouse of something—who is the author of your notes? Your notes will most likely include a combination of material that is owned by Preacher Smith, as well as some original material that you create, such as your interpretation or paraphrase of a comment. You are the author of the notes.

Joint Authorship

Suppose you and a couple of friends gather in your garage on a rainy Saturday afternoon to write a new song. At the end of the session, you have written a song that includes lyrics and musical progressions that each of you contributed. Are you the author? Yes, but not because it was your garage. You are the author of the song because you created it. But you are not the only person who created the song. Each of your friends who contributed to the creation is also an author of the song. The song is a joint work because it was created by multiple authors. For a joint work, each of the authors is a co-owner of that work's copyright.

Let's look at another example. Suppose Pilot Jones is painting a beautiful picture against a canvas sky with his sky writing plane. As he puffs the last bit of smoke out of his plane to finish his creation, you pull out your camera and take a photo. The photo is a tangible medium and is subject to copyright protection. Who owns the copyright for the photograph? Pilot Jones? No. Pilot Jones' creation vanished into the atmosphere minutes later. You are the author of the photograph. You selected the time to shoot the picture, chose the angle of the shot, and set the zoom lens to your liking. You are the owner of the copyright. The photograph is an example of what is called a derivative work.

Ownership of Derivative Works

A derivative work is a work based upon one or more preexisting works. For example, suppose you create a collage of memorable sporting events by cutting pictures out of various sporting magazines and pasting them onto a poster board. Each of the pictures is a preexisting work that is most likely copyrighted. However, your collage qualifies as a work that can be copyrighted because it is a derivative work. And because you are the author of that work, you are the owner of the copyright.

Good Counsel

Being the owner of the copyright for the derivative work does not mean that you can reproduce and sell copies of the work. You may first need to obtain permission from the owners of the preexisting works that are included in the derivative work.

Yours or Your Employer's Copyright?

Under certain circumstances, the creator or originator of a work is not considered the legal author of the work. In such cases, the creator of the work is not the owner of the copyright. There are two main cases of such a scenario:

- Works of the United States government
- Works made for hire

A work of the United States government is a work prepared by an officer or employee of the United States government as part of that person's official duties. In this situation, the creator does not own a copyright in the work. In fact, no one owns the copyright because the document is considered to be in the public domain.

Examples of works of the United States government include:

- Opinions written by federal judges
- Laws written by legislatures
- Memorandums prepared by senators and congressmen

A work made for hire is a work that meets one of two specific requirements

- The work was created by an employee within the scope of employment.
- The work was created under a qualifying contractual agreement.

Employment-Based Works

If your job, employment, or work duties involve the creation of copyrightable works, the copyright for these works is *owned by your employer*. Some examples of employment-based works made for hire include:

- A software program prepared by an employee of a software engineering company

- A user's guide prepared by an employee of a product manufacturing company
- A training manual prepared by a sales company employee and used to teach new employees the company's techniques for selling product
- An article written by an employee of a newspaper publishing company

Is everything that an employee creates considered a work made for hire? Only those works that are created within the scope of the employment are considered works made for hire. For example, suppose an employee of a software engineering company comes up with an idea for a painting while he or she is at work. At closing time, the engineer heads home and puts the idea on canvas. Is this a work made for hire? No! The software engineer's employment includes the creation of software for his company, not the painting of pictures. The employee did not paint the picture on company time or use company equipment. The software engineer would own the copyright to this painting.

Let's look at an example that is a closer call. Suppose that the software engineer's employer is in the business of creating and marketing database management software. While working on a program, the software engineer comes up with a new idea for a computer game. The software engineer creates the game on his or her own time, using his or her own computer. Is the computer game considered a work made for hire? No, it is not.

Are You an Employee?

An important point to understand is that under copyright law, the term employee may not necessarily have the same meaning that is traditionally applied to that term. For the purposes of copyright law, there are at least three factors to consider when determining if a particular person is an employee. These factors include:

- The degree of control the employer has over the work or over the individual creating the work
- The character of the employer's business
- The character of the relationship between the employer and the individual creating the work

In determining whether a person is an employee, the activities of the potential employer and the potential employee are examined in view of these factors. The following list includes various activities of a potential employer that may indicate that an employer-employee relationship exists between a company and a person. So if you are not in a traditional employer-employee relationship, a work you are creating may be considered a work made for hire (and owned by the employer) if the person or entity you are creating the work for performs one or more of the following activities:

- Determines the final format and content of the work.
- Has the work performed at their location.

- Provides the equipment used to create the work.
- Establishes the schedule for creating the work.
- Assigns other tasks to you.
- Hires assistants to help you with the creation of the work.
- Is in the business of producing similar works.
- Provides you with benefits.
- Withholds taxes from your payments.

Work Based on Contract

Even if a person is not considered an employee, a work created by that person may be seen as a work made for hire based on contract law. For a work to be considered a work made for hire on the contractual basis, two conditions must be met:

- There must be a written agreement.
- The work must fall into one of several categories outlined under the copyright law.

The first condition is simple. If there is no written agreement stating that the work you are creating is a work made for hire, then it is not a work made for hire (and, therefore, the creator owns the work). However, if a valid agreement exists, the work that you create must also fall within one of the following categories to be considered a work made for hire:

- A contribution to a collective work
- A part of a motion picture or other audiovisual work

- A translation
- A supplementary work
- A compilation
- An instructional text
- A test
- Answer material for a test
- An atlas

A supplementary work is a work prepared for publication as an addition to or part of a work by another author and used to introduce, conclude, illustrate, explain, revise, comment upon, or assist the other work. Examples of supplementary works include:

- Pictorial illustrations
- Maps
- Editorial notes
- Musical arrangements
- Bibliographies
- Appendixes
- Indexes

In short, if you are preparing a work for another person or entity, you need to do a little investigation to determine if you will own the copyright in that work. Before signing a contract, you should seek advice from an attorney to make sure that you know your rights.

Signing Your Copyright Away

You have seen that the creator or originator of a work owns the copyright in that work unless it is considered a work of the United States government or a work made for hire. However, there are other situations in which you may give up your owner-ship rights to a copyrighted work. These situations always involve a contractual agreement.

A common situation is when a person sells or trans-fers his or her ownership to another person or entity. There are many ways to transfer a copyright own-ership. One typical situation is when the copyright is sold to another entity. This type of a transfer is defined in a signed and written agreement. Another typical situation is when the copyright is transferred to the heirs of the previous owner. This type of a transfer is accomplished through a will or through state law in the absence of a will.

Straight from the Record

In 1985, Michael Jackson purchased the copyright ownership in the Beatles song catalog for $47.5 million and sold half of it to Sony in 1991 for an estimated $100 million.

Another common situation is found in employee or contractor agreements. These agreements typically state that any works made for hire will belong to the company. Oftentimes, these agreements go a step further and state that if you create any works that don't meet the requirements of a work made for hire described above, you still have the obligation to assign your rights in the work to the company.

> **Good Counsel** _____
>
> If you are requested to sign an employee or contractor agreement, you need to realize that you may be forfeiting some of your rights. We strongly recommend hiring an attorney to review such an agreement and advise you regarding the ramifications of signing it.

The Least You Need to Know

- The author of a work is the owner of the copyright.
- If you are creating a work for another person or entity, you should determine whether you are the author by examining the works made for the United States government and the works made for hire rules.
- Owning a copyright for a work does not mean that you are free to copy and sell the work if it is based on other copyrighted works.

Chapter 8

Software Copyrights

In This Chapter

- A definition of software
- The copyright protection available for software
- An overview of the Digital Millennium Copyright Act
- Software piracy
- Protection of computer chips

You may be wondering what exactly this chapter on software copyrights is all about. You use Tupperware extensively and have even hosted a Tupperware party. You go to the hardware store down the road at least twice a month. But what is this software thing all about?

Okay, so here is the ugly definition of software: computer programs, procedures, rules, and possibly associated documentation and data pertaining to the operation of a computer system. And here is a much more user-friendly definition of software: the expression of a computer programmer's idea for a program that runs on a computing device.

In this chapter, we explain the levels of protection that can be obtained for software. This will be of particular interest to the software programmer but it is also important for those who use, copy, or modify ("reverse engineer") software.

Is Software a Hard Concept?

We just provided you with two definitions of software. As a matter of fact, there is no universally agreed-upon definition of software. This makes it a little difficult to determine what kind of copyright protection can be extended to software, doesn't it?

A Closer Look at Copyrightable Software

Software is a relatively new concept. The first computer was introduced in the late 1940s. Copyright law had been around for a very long time before the concept of software came on the scene. If you ever purchased a computer, you have undoubtedly experienced the disappointment when hearing that a newer, smaller, lighter, faster, and less expensive computer has been introduced months, or even weeks later. Technology is advancing so rapidly that the definition of software is constantly changing.

If we really want to wrap our arms around this software concept, we are going to have to look at a few examples to help us determine the definition. But rather than defining the entire world of software, we will focus on a definition of copyrightable software.

Software Defined

You already know that copyright protection is not available for ideas, procedures, processes, systems, methods of operation, concepts, principles, or discoveries. Copyright protection only extends to original expressions. Does this leave any room for software copyright protection at all? Let's look at some examples.

Suppose you wrote a software program that added two numbers together to obtain a sum. Because this is a mathematical principle, the underlying subject matter cannot be copyrighted. But can the program be copyrighted? If the program is an original expression, then it can be protected by copyright. However, the protection is going to be greatly limited. As you recall, copyright protection is not an exclusive right. Another person who independently creates a software program exactly like yours can also have copyright protection if that program is an original expression. A process as simple as adding two numbers together to obtain a sum will have a very limited number of original expressions. For that reason, it would be very difficult to prove that someone actually copied your work.

Let's look at a more involved example. You have decided that you are done with cookbooks. They take up too much counter space, so you decide to write a software program that will allow you to record all of your favorite recipes and recall them to the computer screen. In addition, you can generate grocery shopping lists based on required ingredients, sort the recipes based on cuisines or ingredients, and display helpful hints along with the recipe to assist you in selecting complementary side dishes and wines. Can this software program be protected by copyright? Certainly. What is not protected is the individual listing of ingredients for each recipe; however, the program as a whole can be protected under copyright law.

Suppose that someone else wanted to write a program similar to your recipe program. In fact, someone else can write a program that functions and operates identically without violating your copyright protection. The underlying operations of your program are not protected by copyright law; what is protected by copyright is just the software program written to perform these functions.

The term software was first introduced to separate things that were hardware from things that were not. Before the introduction of programmable computers, machines designed to perform certain tasks were made only of hardware. An example is a mechanical typewriter. Back in the old days, we actually had a machine with keys that, when pressed, would make a letter-shaped anvil bang against an ink-soaked ribbon to result in placing a typed letter on a piece of paper. Today we are more familiar with a computer that includes a word processor program which creates computer documents that are sent to a printer. The mechanical typewriter is an example of a hardware-only device. The word processor program is an example of software. A general rule of thumb is that hardware cannot be reprogrammed while software can.

Straight from the Record

The No Electronic Theft Act closed a loophole under old laws that allowed people to distribute commercial software over the Internet without facing prosecution. Today it is a crime to do so even if the offender is not profiting from these actions.

What else can be considered software? Can the contents of a music CD or a movie on DVD be considered software? What about video games? The answer is yes; each of these items can also be considered as software. The music CD contains information that a CD player reads and converts into musical signals. This is very similar to a software program that includes instructions for a computer. Throughout this chapter, we make references to these special forms of software; for more details on music, movie, and online copyrights refer to Chapters 9, 10, and 11.

The Form of Software

What forms of software are protected under copyright law? This concept can get pretty technical but we keep it simple for you. A software program can be printed onto paper, stored on a magnetic disk, stored on a CD, or another recordable medium. Software can exist in the form of instructions that you can read with your eye or it can be translated into a computer language. If you are a technology person, the terms that come to mind are source code, object code, machine code, flowcharts, and so on. But don't be dismayed, we already explained that any physical form of a copyrighted work can be protected. So regardless of the form, if the software can be protected by copyright, the protection will extend to any of these physical forms.

Earlier in this chapter we described the difference between hardware and software. There is also a form that exists between hardware and software—firmware. Firmware is a term used to describe software that is embedded into a computing device and not intended to be modified. Generally speaking, firmware is a form of software that has been stored onto a computer chip and cannot be modified by a computer user. Thus, firmware is a program that is neither "hard" nor "soft."

DCMA—Digital Millennium Copyright Act

In 1998 a very extensive amendment was made to the Copyright Act. This amendment is called the Digital Millennium Copyright Act, or DMCA. In the early 1990s, it became apparent that the growth in the computer industry, especially the widespread use of the World Wide Web or the Internet, was resulting in some very complicated copyright issues. A task force in the United States conducted a review of the problems arising in the digital age and the protections available under the copyright laws at that time. The task force determined that current

U.S. copyright law was a pretty decent fit for handling most of the important copyright issues that concerned software, otherwise called *digital content*. However, it was also clear that there were some very serious holes that needed substantial mending. The task force proposed several recommendations; some of the more important ones are included in the following list:

- Expanding the exclusive rights of copyright owners to include the right of transmission. (This recommendation was included because technology allows content to be transferred so easily.)

- Updating the library exemption to permit making three copies of a work and allowing digital as well as facsimile copies.

- Creating new prohibitions on devices or services designed to circumvent mechanisms which protect the rights of copyright owners and which affect newly recognized copyright management information.

- Establishing a new limitation on reproduction to help the visually impaired.

After many meetings, hearings, and debates on this subject, the United States enacted the Digital Millennium Copyright Act in 1998. The purpose of the Digital Millennium Copyright Act was to fill in the holes of the Copyright Act to make it more applicable to the digital age. Some of the key provisions of the Digital Millennium Copyright Act are summarized in the following section along with the relationship of these provisions to software copyright protection.

Aar! It Be a Hard Life for a Pirate, Ye Know?

The Digital Millennium Copyright act made it a crime to circumvent antipiracy measures built into most commercial software. What is antipiracy? Piracy refers to the illegal copying and distribution of software. Similar to the pirates of old, software pirates steal and plunder from the works of others for their own benefit. Antipiracy measures are taken by software programmers, manufactures, and distributors to prevent or limit the ability to make illegal copies of software.

An example of a common antipiracy measure is the use of unique product codes by Microsoft Corporation. During the installation process of a Microsoft product, the user is required to enter a series of numbers and letters that are obtained from the software packaging. This measure provides some level of protection in that the pirate not only requires a copy of the software, but also the product code. Microsoft has recently improved this antipiracy measure by having the product automatically registered with Microsoft over the Internet during the installation process. Now when the product code is entered, Microsoft is notified of the software installation and the product code can be disabled for future installations of the software.

Under the Digital Millennium Copyright Act, if a person does anything to circumvent the antipiracy measures, he or she can be charged with criminal conduct. Such actions include creating code-cracking programs that allow for the copying and installation of software programs.

There is an exception to this provision. As long as a person is operating in a good-faith manner, he or she is permitted to circumvent antipiracy measures. What is a good-faith manner? It includes activities related to encryption research, assessing product inter-operability, and testing computer security.

Straight from the Record

The Digital Millennium Copyright Act has a special provision that provides copyright protection for the design of a vessel hull. So just in case you're thinking of copying your favorite cruise ship and selling miniature models, beware! You could be infringing on a copyright.

Internet Service Providers

The Digital Millennium Act provides some level of comfort for Internet service providers (ISPs). An Internet service provider is a company that provides you with access to the Internet. Tons and tons of information can be passed through the computers owned and operated by an Internet service provider. The Digital Millennium Act limits Internet service providers from copyright infringement liability for simply transmitting information over the Internet.

This limitation is important because it would be an impossible burden, at least from a commercial perspective, for the Internet service provider to examine each item of information passing through its computer systems and then block anything that is protected by copyright. In fact, it would most likely bring the Internet to a screeching halt.

Internet service providers are not totally free and clear, however. Typically, an ISP will provide memory allocations for users to host their websites on the ISP's computers. The ISPs have the responsibility to monitor their users' websites and remove material that appears to constitute copyright infringement.

Library Liability

The Digital Millennium Copyright Act expanded some of the copyright exceptions available to libraries. You should know, however, that libraries mentioned in the copyright law do not include your personal library at home. The library exemptions only apply to public libraries and to materials made available to the public in those libraries. One of the expansions is that a library can obtain a copy of a commercially exploited copyrighted work to evaluate whether it should be included in the inventory. The library can only use the copyrighted work for a reasonable period of time it takes to conduct the evaluation and it cannot use the work for any other purposes.

Another expansion in the copyright law is to make the rules related to archived copies for libraries more reasonable. A library can now maintain three copies of certain items. One copy can be used strictly for archival purposes, another copy can be distributed to the public, and the third copy can be used as a replacement should the publicly distributed copy become damaged.

The Semiconductor Chip Protection Act

Another form of copyright protection is available for a class of works that includes mask works or semiconductors. These works fall into a category that is between software and hardware. One could describe the works in this category as programmable hardware. Let's look at a couple of definitions.

A mask work is defined as a series of related images, however fixed or encoded, that fulfills these two conditions:

- It has or represents the predetermined three-dimensional pattern of metallic, insulating, or semiconductor material present or removed from the layers of a semiconductor chip product.

- The relation of the images to one another is that each image has the pattern of the surface of one form of the semiconductor chip product.

A semiconductor, or integrated circuit, is defined as the final or intermediate form of any product that:

- Has two or more layers of metallic, insulating, or semiconductor material that is either deposited, placed on, etched away, or removed from a piece of semiconductor material in accordance with a predetermined pattern.

- Is intended to perform electronic circuitry functions.

Now let's take this down a notch. In general, a mask work is a set of instructions that tell a machine how to create a specific semiconductor. Although the mask work has purely functional features, in contrast with most copyright law, they are protected by copyright. However, to be protected, the design of a mask work must not be dictated solely by a particular electronic function and it must not be one of only a few available design choices that will accomplish that function.

The Least You Need to Know

- Software programs are protected under copyright law; the underlying functions of the software are not protected by copyright law.

- The Digital Millennium Copyright Act is a change to the copyright law that works to modernize the current rules to encompass recent advancements in technology.

- Software piracy can result in criminal liability for making illegal copies of software and also for defeating antipiracy protections that have been included in the software.

- Semiconductors, although technically not software, can also be protected under the Semiconductor Chip Protection Act.

Chapter 9

Music Copyrights

In This Chapter

- Understanding music as a copyrighted work
- Making sure you're not caught pirating music
- Playing millions of tunes for one low, low price

We've spent some time talking about copyrights as they might apply to any number of subject areas. One of the most critical areas of copyrights is the creation and distribution of music.

Whether you're a musician or a lover of music, it's important to become familiar with the copyrights as they apply to music. As a musician, you need to make sure that others protect your rights and also that you don't accidentally infringe another musician's work. As a music lover, you must resist the temptation of grabbing music off the Internet.

We've all heard of ASCAP and BMI, but do you really know what they do? We fill in your knowledge gap so you can impress your friends at the next party (while they're listening to great music blasting over a stereo).

Déjà Vu All Over Again?

A copyright is a copyright. Therefore, all the rules and approaches you've learned throughout this book equally apply to music. In some cases, music gets even more protection. So why are we taking up your time? Because, thanks to technology advances in our society, we need to spend some extra time explaining the peculiarities of music copyrights.

Different Strokes for Different Folks

If this chapter is of particular interest to you, you are probably a musician, someone who loves music, or someone who loves music so much that you try to obtain as much music as possible without paying for it.

For Aspiring Musicians

So you want to be a rock 'n' roll star? If you're coming up with wonderful songs and want to make sure that you're adequately protected, we highly recommend that you follow the registration procedures outlined in this book. In doing so, you will be assured that if anybody infringes your songs, you can demonstrate that you took appropriate measures to protect your work and you can seek statutory damages. Remember, music can fall into two categories—the category of a sound recording or the category of a performing arts work. The person who writes the song and lyrics (the music sheets) can register it as a performing arts work (since it is intended to be performed). The recorded music should be registered as a sound recording, unless it accompanies an audiovisual work, such as a movie, in which case it can be registered as a performing arts work.

Infringement as a Songwriter

As a songwriter, you should be very careful about incorporating pieces or larger components of others' music, lyrics, or other elements into your songs. Much of the copyright litigation over the years has involved one artist suing another for infringement. As you may recall from Chapter 3, when reviewing a case of potential infringement, the test is to establish access to the original work and substantial similarity. Given the ease of transmission on the Internet, access to a particular song is fairly easy to prove, assuming that the song has been made generally available. The similarity of two songs can be demonstrated from an overall perspective (for example, if the songs sound very similar and have similar lyrics), or you can listen to parts or layers of the song. For example, a song may have a particular beat, or a repeated guitar riff or lyric. One example of this is Ray Parker, Jr.'s song "Ghostbusters." Huey Lewis sued Parker, alleging that Parker incorporated the background rhythm of Lewis' song "I wanna new drug" into "Ghostbusters." Lewis won the claim.

> **Straight from the Record**
>
> In Vanilla Ice's hit "Ice Ice Baby," it was alleged that Vanilla Ice lifted David Bowie's most recognized riffs from "Under Pressure" and inserted them into his song. Suits were threatened and rumor has it that the parties settled out of court.

For Aspiring File Sharers and Bootleggers

How times are a changin'! It used to be so easy to be a music pirate. Simply get on the Web, find your favorite music, and download it. Music is especially susceptible to piracy since digital music files are small (compared to video files) and easy to identify on the Web because they are categorized under common song names. Also, the music industry does a great job of promoting its artists and making many people interested in getting the music. The clincher is that popular music is loved by the younger generation that understands the technology needed to share the music all too well. Because of these factors, the music industry is extremely focused on eliminating what they consider to be music piracy.

Napster and the Like

By now, you've likely heard of Napster. Although Napster in its original form is now defunct, other similar services still exist. These services are called peer-to-peer music file-sharing systems. Through your computer, you're able to search the web for someone who possesses a song that you want on their computer. If that person has compatible file-sharing software, you can simply grab the song off the person's computer and download (or record) it to your computer. As you might imagine, the record companies who have spent an exorbitant amount of money recording and promoting a particular artist's music in hopes of you purchasing it are adamantly against these file-sharing services.

Is your download of a song using file-sharing software considered copyright infringement? The courts have found that it is. And remember that your download of these songs could result in statutory monetary damages of up to $25,000 for each song! You can do the math. But should you worry? Will you ever be sued?

Straight from the Record

Sean Fanning wrote the software code and started Napster at the age of 18, when he was a freshman at Boston's Northeastern University. By the time he turned 19, he was a household name and the target of lawsuits by all the major record companies.

The Recording Industry Association of America

It's worth a moment to tell you a bit about the Recording Industry Association of America (RIAA), an organization at the forefront of the music copyright infringement wars. The RIAA counts among its members all the major record labels and a tremendous number of smaller labels. The stated mission of the RIAA is "to foster a business and legal climate that supports and promotes our members' creative and financial vitality." As such, it has taken a very aggressive stance toward infringement. You can learn more about the RIAA at www.riaa.com.

The RIAA filed suit and prevailed against companies like Napster. The RIAA could target Napster because all of the transfer activity went through Napster's computer systems. Therefore, as their theory went, if you shut down Napster, the service goes away. Unfortunately (or fortunately, depending on your views), companies developed new technologies that did not require a "middle-man" company such as Napster. You can simply transfer the music to and from another individual directly as long as you both have compatible software. As a result, millions of people are currently transferring music to one another and it's extremely difficult for the RIAA and record companies to identify infringements.

That being said, the RIAA is striking back. It has filed many lawsuits against individuals who are illegally downloading and sharing music files. The RIAA believes that this campaign will educate the public about copyright infringement and deter would-be infringers.

Objections

Be careful! One of the individuals sued by the RIAA was a 65-year-old grandmother. She claimed she was falsely accused and the RIAA dropped the lawsuit. However, it shows that the RIAA is willing to sue any individual deemed to have infringed copyrights owned by its members.

Bootlegging

It has been an object of concertgoers since the early days of recording devices to capture their favorite acts on tape. Problem is that taping concerts without approval is a violation of the Uruguay Round Agreements Act. In 1994, President Clinton signed this act, which prohibited the recording of live musical performances (known as *bootlegs*) even if there was no separate recordation of the performance. There are also provisions in the act for distributing or transmitting a bootlegged copy of a concert (so the guy selling copies in the parking lot after the show could be targeted as well). However, even though this smells like copyright law, it really isn't and violation of the act is not copyright infringement. This is really a separate act that takes care of a loophole in the copyright law.

Straight from the Record

The Grateful Dead, a band that started in San Francisco in the 1960s and ended upon lead singer Jerry Garcia's death in the late 1990s, welcomed recording devices into their concerts. They believed that the sharing of their music would build a community of fans, commonly known as Deadheads.

Legal Approaches

Do you have to commit a crime to get digital music? No! Many music services have developed over the last several years that enable you to legally download individual songs and albums of your favorite artists. These services are run by a variety of companies, from the record companies themselves to independent music services and computer manufacturers such as Apple Computer and its online iTunes music store.

Digital Rights Management

Certain software companies have developed (and will continue to improve) software known as digital rights management (or DRM) technology. DRM technology is aimed at protecting content from illegal digital transfer. For example, a DRM technique might be to degrade the audio quality of illegally transferred music upon digital transmission. Other techniques may include the simple inability to transfer the music, or a limited number of times a particular song can be played before it becomes locked and cannot be played further. These companies recognize the value of music content and have developed these programs to limit the extent of copyright infringement.

Getting Comfy Under Blanket Licenses

You may be wondering how radio stations, department stores, on-hold systems, and others play song after song after song. Do they enter into a license agreement for each song? No! They actually have a license either with the American Society of Composers, Authors and Publishers (known as ASCAP), or with BMI. ASCAP claims 170,000 and BMI 300,000 U.S. composers, songwriters, lyricists, and music publishers.

One thing to note is that the members of ASCAP are not necessarily the artists who sing the songs. They are the composers—the individuals who write the music and lyrics. You may recall an exception to the exclusive rights of a copyright holder—performance of a sound recording is not copyright infringement. That means radio stations are free to play recorded music and the recording artist cannot claim infringement. But, without a license from ASCAP or BMI, the individual who wrote the song could prevail in a suit. Therefore, these artists are the beneficiaries of the licensing royalties that ASCAP and BMI generate.

How Blanket Licenses Work

Artists can join ASCAP or BMI and, in doing so, permit these organizations to manage licensing relationships with organizations that want to utilize the artists' music. BMI and ASCAP require methods for tracking the use of songs by these organizations and then charge them based on a rate schedule. When ASCAP and BMI receive royalties from their customers, they allocate this money among the various works that were played by the customers based on how often a particular song was played.

Don't be fooled though. These organizations are not negotiating your licensing relationship for you. They aggregate all of these performing arts works and then enter into "blanket licenses," which means an organization can play any one of the millions of works without negotiating a separate license.

So what kinds of companies enter into licenses with BMI and ASCAP? They include television and radio stations, websites, colleges and universities, restaurants, night clubs, fitness and health clubs, hotels, trade show organizers, amusement parks, airlines, retail stores, concert organizers, and shopping centers and malls, just to name a few! What do all of these organizations have in common? They are largely organizations that cater to the general public and, by having the right to play music (when you're strolling through the mall, for example), they make your experience with them better!

With respect to music, BMI and ASCAP are the primary players. Other forms of copyrighted work have similar associations, such as the motion picture industry.

The Least You Need to Know

- Music is typically protected as a performing arts work (if you're a composer) or as a sound recording (if you record your audio performance of the work).

- Music piracy is a growing concern of record companies and they are taking significant measures to prosecute those who illegally share and download music.

- It is possible to obtain a blanket license if you're interested in playing music for your customers.

Chapter 10

The Silver Screen and TV

In This Chapter

- Copyright protection for movies and television shows
- The rights of the viewer and the creator
- The ramifications of recording broadcasted content
- Showing recorded material to others

It was not so long ago that a young engineer at RCA by the name of Earl E. Masterson wrought havoc in the television broadcast, filming, and taping industries. Although probably not solely responsible, the technology that was invented by this engineer, and the subject of a 1950 patent entitled Magnetic Recording of High Frequency Signals, was a key advancement that led to the development of the video cassette recorder (VCR).

RCA did not realize the significance of this invention and gave up their exclusive rights to the technology in a patent exchange with a company called Ampex. Later, JVC got rights to the patent and developed the first video cassette recorder.

How did this invention impact the television broadcast, filming, and taping industries? All of a sudden, individuals started recording movies, television shows, sporting events, commercials, and other content that was being broadcast to televisions across the nation. The individuals could then play it back anytime, make alterations by skipping commercials, and show it to others. The industry quickly realized they relinquished a huge amount of control over the content. How were the broadcast stations to attract advertisers if the size of the viewing audience dropped suddenly and dramatically? How were broadcasters to convince filming companies to air their movies if the movies could be copied by hundreds of thousands of people? How could the rights of the copyright holders be protected?

In this chapter, we discuss this revolutionary advancement in technology and its effect on copyright law.

Protection Approach

Let's first take a look at what kind of television and motion picture content is protected by copyright laws. As you have learned so far, the filming of a movie, television show, sporting event, commercial, or other similar event can be protected under copyright law. You must have seen the FBI warning that appears at the beginning of a movie you have rented (or bought on VHS or DVD) stating that it is illegal to make copies of the movie that you are about to view.

With the advent of devices that can record television broadcasts, the owners of such copyrighted materials became quite concerned. They were not alone; the music industry had already been confronted with the same issue upon the introduction of the 8-track tape recorder, and later the cassette recorder. And before this, the printing industry confronted the issue when the ability to create photocopies was introduced.

There certainly appears to be a competing interest in our world. The copyright laws want to protect authors so they will be encouraged to create works. However, with valuable advancements in technology, including the VCR, digital recorders, and the like, how can this protection be assured? It is certain that we don't want to limit the advancements in technology. Imagine a world without VCRs. For one thing, there would be quite a few living rooms without a flashing 12:00 on the VCR screen. However, the detriments to society would be huge.

Copyright protection is still available for content that has been broadcast over a television station or delivered to a home or office through a cable system. Similar to the advent of the photocopier and the cassette recorder, the VCR has not caused a collapse in the underlying content creation industry. Instead, it has simply encouraged the copyright laws to be tightened and the invention of technology that can be used to prevent unauthorized copying of content.

What Are the Viewer's Rights?

Let's say your favorite television show airs at 5:30 P.M. on Tuesdays right when you are stuck in the middle of rush hour traffic and desperately trying to get home. So you purchased a VCR and figured out how to program it. The wonderful world of technology has enabled you to relax while you sit in traffic, knowing that you can comfortably watch your favorite program later that evening, unless your spouse or children have messed up the VCR. By recording the show, are you violating copyright law?

The answer is no—fortunately for you. The copyright law states that such use is not an infringement. More specifically, the copyright law states that you can record a transmission of a performance, such as a movie or television show, onto a single receiving device of the kind that is commonly used in private homes. So you can relax while you watch your favorite TV show without fear that the FBI is going to knock on your door and drag you off to the pokey.

There are some very serious and significant limitations to your rights though. One of these limitations is that you are not allowed to charge others to see or hear the content that you recorded. In other words, you can't record your favorite show and then charge your buddies $1.00 to watch it at your house. This also applies if you make recordings of an entire television series. You can't throw a Bob's favorite shows party and charge your friends, relatives, or others to stop by and view it.

Another limitation is that you are not allowed to further transmit the recorded program to the public. For example, if you own a bar or a restaurant, you are not allowed to play copies of the content that you've recorded for the patrons of the bar or restaurant.

But are there any fuzzy areas regarding this issue? Certainly. Suppose you have a club that meets periodically. At one of the meetings, you decide to show a movie that you previously recorded. Is this a violation of copyright law? It can be. To determine the correct answer you have to do a little bit of measuring, a little bit of counting, and get permission.

In general, the copyright laws allow you to show recorded or broadcasted content to the public if you meet certain criteria. The criteria has to do with the size of the building or establishment in which you are showing the content, the number of speakers used, and the number of screens used for displaying the content. We won't get into the specifics of these measurements and counts because, at the end of the day, you are still required to meet the following three criteria:

- You cannot charge others to see or hear the content.

- You cannot further transmit the content beyond the establishment.

- Most important, the transmission of the content must be licensed by the copyright owner.

Straight from the Record _____

Just to give you an idea of establishment sizes and speaker/display counts, here are the numbers. Except for bars or restaurants, you are limited to a space of 2,000 square feet in size. If the space is more than 2,000 square feet, you are limited to no more than 4 display devices with only 1 allowed per room, with no display greater than 55 inches diagonally, and no more than 6 speakers with a maximum of 4 speakers per room.

You may be wondering at this point why the other factors are important if you still need a license from the copyright owner. A key purpose of the provision is that a creator can provide content to the public but still maintain some level of control over its viewing.

For example, a company may desire others to view a certain program but to limit such viewings in order to ensure some sales of the original program. By limiting the size of the establishment, the number of speakers, the number of displays, or the like, the content creator can ensure that the program won't be viewed by thousands of people sitting in a huge auditorium.

There are also exceptions for displaying audiovisual content for educational purposes.

Straight from the Record

It is perfectly legal for you to purchase a DVD or VCR tape in another country and bring it back to the United States for your personal use. However, you are not allowed to buy 100 copies, bring them back to the United States and sell them to others.

What Are the Creator's Rights?

Audiovisual works are protected by copyright laws. Other than the allowed actions described above, the copyright owner of an audiovisual work has the right to limit the transmission, viewing, and dissemination of the work.

As with other copyright infringements, it is not always easy to police the marketplace for copyright infringers. However, the copyright laws provide very good and stringent measures for copyright violators.

Suppose the owner of a copyrighted work has authorized the work to be viewed or retransmitted in accordance with the limitations identified above. Does this have an adverse effect on the royalties the owner can collect? Can an infringer argue that such authorization should limit the amount of damages to be imposed on the infringer? The answer to these questions is: no. The copyright law specifically states that the exceptions will not be taken into account when setting or adjusting the royalty payments due to a copyright owner for the public performance or display of their work.

> **Straight from the Record**
>
> If you want to show content in a restaurant or bar, here are the specific measurements of concern. You are limited to a space of 3,750 square feet in size. If the space is greater than 3,750 square feet, you are limited to no more than 4 display devices with only 1 allowed per room, no display can be greater than 55 inches diagonally, and no more than 6 speakers with a maximum of 4 speakers per room.

Copyright Challenges: VCR and TIVO

As technology continues to advance, additional copyright issues will certainly surface in this area. We focused primarily on the VCR because it was the first introduction into the audiovisual recording technology. But with more recent advances, these issues have become more prominent.

Digital, Let's Get Digital

One significant issue that the television and movie industries were grateful for was the substantial decrease in quality of a VCR recording versus cable broadcasts or silver screen movies. However, with the rise of digital technology, the quality of a recording can greatly compete with the quality available on the silver screen. This made the industry a bit more nervous.

Straight from the Record

The Motion Picture Association of America (MPAA) and its international counterpart, the Motion Picture Association (MPA), estimate that the U.S. motion picture industry loses in excess of $3 billion annually in potential worldwide revenue due to piracy.

The digital video (or digital versatile) disk provides great improvement in the quality of a recorded audiovisual work. As the prices of DVD recorders drop, individuals can create perfect quality copies of copyrighted DVDs. For example, similar to VCR to VCR recording, with DVD recorders, an individual can make an exact replica of a DVD that was rented from the local movie rental store. It is important to point out that such a recording is not allowed under copyright law. The direct recording of a rented movie is not the same as recording of a transmission and it is a violation of copyright law.

Do You TiVo?

It is predicted that the video cassette and even the DVD industry will be greatly impacted by a newer technology—the personal video recorders (PVRs). PVRs are essentially VCRs on steroids. Audiovisual content is recorded to a hard disk inside the device. The fact that the PVR is essentially a computer allows for a great deal of flexibility in recording, sharing, and manipulating the content on the hard disk.

Straight from the Record

Several commercial products are available that enable you to copy a DVD onto a CD device. You should engage in such activity with great fear and trembling. Although copyright law has established that you can make copies of items that you purchase for personal use, the Digital Millennium Copyright Act has made it illegal to circumvent copy protection measures. Thus, using such products may be a direct violation of copyright law even if you copy an item that you have purchased.

Once again, the TV and movie industries view PVRs as a significant threat to their business and are seeking ways to limit use and features of these devices. For example, the Motion Picture Association of America sued SonicBlue, a now bankrupt company, over a feature that enables consumers to delete commercials from the content they record.

Straight from the Record

A practice that is taking place today is for people to sneak a video camera into a preview of a movie that has not yet been released, record the movie using the camera, and then make the movie available on the Internet. Beware that obtaining such bootleg copies of a movie is a violation of the copyright law.

The Future

Further advances will undoubtedly take place in recording technology. These devices will be regulated continually by the U.S. government to ensure that the rights of the copyright holders are not violated. In addition, technological advances will continue in the areas of antipiracy and copy protection. The copyright laws have recently been modified to make it a criminal act to circumvent any measures that have been put in place to prevent copying of copyrighted material.

Straight from the Record

Copyright violation is a serious offense. The unauthorized copy or sale of copyrighted movies with a retail value exceeding $2,500 is a felony and brings five years in jail, without parole, and a $250,000 fine.

The Least You Need to Know

- Content that is broadcast through the airwaves or cables can be copyrighted material that is protected under the law.
- As a viewer, you have certain rights to copy broadcast content but they are limited to personal uses.

- You cannot publicly display recorded content or charge a fee for viewing it if the content is protected by copyright law.
- Violations of copyright laws can be very costly and result in prison time.

11

Online Copyrights

In This Chapter

- What exactly is online content?
- The protection and registration of online content
- What to watch out for if you create a website
- What uses of online content are permissible
- Recent changes pertaining to Internet service providers

Was it really Al Gore who invented the Internet? We may never know the answer to that question but one thing is for certain—the creation of the Internet resulted in many issues regarding copyright protection of content—namely online content.

When copyright law was first created, it was built around a concept of writings on paper. The ability to photocopy did not even exist at that time. But as technology advanced throughout the years, copyright law has been running like a head with its chicken cut off to keep up with it.

One of the more recent changes in copyright law has been in the area of online copyrights. There are many interesting issues surrounding this topic and many more will continue to surface. The most important question is whether the copyrighted content that you put on the Internet is still protected by copyright law. For example, if the material is accessible via the Internet from your server, then whenever it is accessed by a web browser or other web application, a copy of the material will be created in the cache file allocated to the web browser. This cache file exists on the hard drive of the computer running the web browser. Thus, a copy of the material will exist on that hard drive until the cache file is erased or purged. In addition, a copy of the material will be created on every computer on the Internet path between your server and the computer accessing the file. If your material is copyrighted, then has your copyright just been violated or is the world free to copy your online content?

Another interesting issue is a copyright notice. Traditionally, a copyright notice is included as part of the protected work. For example, look at the front pages of this book and you will see a copyright notice. Likewise, authors of online content include a copyright notice within the online content. But wait a minute here! In order to get the notice that online content is protected by copyright laws, you have to access that very content with your computer. You have already copied the copyrighted work just to get the notice. How do you protect your online content and provide adequate copyright notice to the surfers of the world? This chapter reviews the current copyright laws that relate to online documents. As you read through, you will find the answers to the questions we raised in this introduction, as well as many other questions regarding the copyright of online content.

Is Online Content Protected by Copyright?

Before we answer this question, let's first get our arms around the concept of online content. When we refer to online content, we are talking about items that can be accessed via the Internet or other wide or local area networks.

For example, when you launch your web browser and type in www.lavagroup.net, your computer screen will display the website of this book's authors. Everything that you see inside your browser window is considered online content. Online content includes the text, the graphics, the clip art images, and the layout of the web page. But that's not all. What you see in the browser window is the result of a software program reading a special computer language and interpreting that language to create the displayed content. That language is most commonly referred to as hypertext markup language or HTML. What's important is that the content displayed by your browser as well as the computer language file can be protected by copyright.

Have you ever loaded a website that includes animation or moving objects? These items are usually created in computer languages other than HTML.

When you access a website that includes such content, a program gets loaded into your computer and begins running. The program that creates the animation or moving objects can also be protected by copyright.

So can online content be protected by copyright laws? You bet your britches! The same rules that are used to determine if other content can be protected by copyright also apply to online content. This is good news, right? Once you go through all the effort to create a website, it is nice to know that it is protected under copyright laws. However, what many people don't realize is that copying online content from other websites and incorporating it into your website can be a copyright infringement.

For example, let's say you just came back from a trip to Hawaii and decide to create a web page that includes pictures from your trip along with descriptions of the places you visited. You also decide to add some pictures or graphics that you copied from the website of one of the hotels you stayed at. In addition, you want to have your website play the Hawaii Five-O theme song—the version by the Brian Setzer Orchestra, of course. Guess what? If you do those things, you may be a copyright infringer.

Copyright Protection for Online Content

There are at least three different perspectives that you may be curious about regarding copyright protection of online content:

- You want to protect and own the content on your website.

- You want to learn what content you can use on your website or for other purposes without infringing someone else's copyrights.

- You may provide web hosting services to others and you want to know your potential risks of copyright infringement.

Let's take a look at these issues.

Wrapping Up Your Content

As you have already learned, any original expression that you put into a physical form is protected under copyright laws. Online content qualifies as a physical form and is therefore protected. So if you create a website for yourself, you own the copyrights in that online content.

Suppose you want a website but you don't have the technical expertise to create one yourself. Just run a quick search on the Internet and you will find thousands of companies that are in the business of creating websites for a fee. But be careful! If you hire a company to create a website for you, you may not be the copyright owner of the website. The concept of a work made for hire applies in the context of creating websites.

Let's look at the process of creating a website. You call up the ACME Website Creation Company and hire them to create a website. You have a good idea of what you want but don't know how to make it happen, so you work closely with the designer. In the process, you create several textual excerpts that you want to include on the website; you may even provide some graphics or pictures. The designer is creating other content such as graphics and text, laying out the various items in a particular manner, and adding other decorative features. Clearly, the items that you provide to the designer are your creations and you own the copyright in those items. However, the designer owns the copyright in pretty much everything else—even the HTML file.

How can this be remedied? If you hire a company to create your website, they will most likely be considered an independent contractor. If you want to own the online content, the HTML, and all the other related items, you need to make sure that your agreement with ACME Website Creation Company specifically states that you will own the copyrights. But be ready for a negotiation battle. Website designers often like to re-use items that they've created for other clients. Thus, the website designer may be unwilling to sign away all of the copyrights in the final product.

Good Counsel

If you are considering putting a photo of someone else (for example, a model) on your website, or if your web designer makes such a suggestion, you need to make sure that you obtain a copy of the model release. The model release will indicate whether the model allows you to use the photo.

The Fine Art of Using Online Content

You should always assume that anything you find on the Internet is copyrighted. Even if there is no copyright notice, it may still be protected. Whether you are obtaining online content to include in your website, a presentation you are preparing, or a document you are writing, make sure you use any such content with great caution. You should treat online content in exactly the same way you would treat a reference book, a journal, or a magazine.

Many websites on the Internet may advertise that their content is not protected by copyright and that it can be freely used by others. You should still be very cautious. Just because a website states that its content can be freely used, they may be unknowingly or knowingly offering items that are someone else's.

What uses are permitted? Well, you can certainly relax and surf the Web without fear that any page you load is an infringement of someone else's copyright. Any content that is made accessible on the Internet is published and you have the right to read it, view it, and enjoy it. But you can't copy it. However, the copy of the file that is loaded into your computer is not considered a copyright infringement.

Suppose you find an interesting website and want to send a link to the website to a friend. Is this considered a case of copyright infringement? Or let's say you want to create a website and include several links to sites that are owned by others. Would this be deemed an infringement of copyright? Like we mentioned earlier, the copyright law is still trying to catch up with technology so there is no definitive answer to these questions. Your best bet is to always get permission if in doubt.

The Hostess with the Mostest

If you are a web host or an Internet service provider (ISP), the recent changes in copyright laws should help you sleep much better at night. You have now read about the Digital Millennium Copyright Act in relationship to software copyrights. The Digital Millennium Copyright Act includes a very lengthy section that focuses specifically on the rights of service providers. We won't go into detail on all of the nice changes that Congress has made in this act—after all, this *is* a *Pocket Idiot's Guide* and even the largest of pockets have a limited size.

The biggest concern for ISPs is that a large amount of online content passes through, gets stored within, and gets retransmitted by their systems. This sounds a lot like the activity of a copyright infringer. However, you can imagine that even Al Gore's Internet would come to a screeching halt if ISPs were restricted from such activity.

The Digital Millennium Copyright Act defines an ISP as a service that provides online content between points on the Internet without modifying the content, or a provider of online services or network access.

Under the current copyright law, ISPs are not in danger of being liable for copyright infringement for delivery or transmission of copyrighted material under the following conditions:

- The transmission of the material is not initiated by the service provider.
- The transmission is carried out through an automatic technical process.
- The service provider does not select the recipient of the material.
- The copies of the material on the service provider's equipment are only temporary.
- The service provider does not modify the content.

Thus, ISPs that are simply operating in the manner they're accustomed to can do so without fear of losing a suit for copyright infringement.

Copyright Registration

We have already covered the copyright registration process in great detail. However, there are a few issues related specifically to online content that we discuss in this section.

What kind of online content should you register with the U.S. Copyright Office? As you now know, the content on a website can include many different items. You first need to determine what it is you want to protect. Is it just the text, the graphics, or the entire display of the website? To obtain the most widespread protection, you should submit all of these things for copyright registration. For example, if you simply submit printouts of the HTML code for your website, you will only obtain protection for that specific code. If someone else creates a very similar page using different HTML code, they may not be violating your copyright. If you can muddle through the process of registering your copyrights on your own—that is without using a lawyer—the process is quite economical. And relatively speaking, even if you use a lawyer, the cost of filing for copyright protection should not be too outlandish. Just make sure you shop for the right lawyer.

What should you submit to the copyright office along with your request for registration? Well, don't send a CD-ROM packed full of web pages. The copyright office is trying to modernize their processes but they still require and prefer printed copies of your content. Thus, you should prepare printouts of each page of your website to submit for registration, as well as a printout of the HTML code. If your website includes JavaScript or any other scripting language, you should print out the source code and submit it to the copyright office.

Straight from the Record

One of the most well-known websites on the Internet is Yahoo!. And guess what?! They don't register their content with the copyright office. Their position is that the content of their website changes so frequently, it would take too much effort to keep the registrations up-to-date.

Copyright Infringement

Copyright infringement is a serious matter and the infringement of online content is an easy stumbling block. Online content is so readily available and so easily copied that even the most straight-laced person could accidentally become an infringer. You should take care any time you are creating online content or using anything that you obtain from the Internet. If you have any doubts, you should always seek advice.

If you're ever thinking to yourself, "It is just little ole me, they will never find me and discover my infringement," beware! Many companies are now offering services that search through the Internet looking for copyright infringers and copyrighted material. These companies can identify infringements by companies, as well as individuals.

The Least You Need to Know

- Online content can be quite varied and includes the items that you see through a web browser, as well as the underlying computer instructions that you don't see.

- Online content is protected through the copyright laws.

- If you are creating a website or utilizing online content from other websites, you should make sure that you are not infringing someone else's copyrights.

- Recent changes in the copyright laws have greatly limited the liability of Internet service providers for copyright infringement.

Chapter 12

Final Copyright Need-to-Knows

In This Chapter

- Treading international waters
- Copyrights and the Web
- Swimming with the sharks (lawyers)

We've covered a ton about copyrights in a pocket guide. However, there are a few more items that are worth mentioning before you're a self-proclaimed copyright expert.

First, we want to cover some foreign ground as it relates to copyrights. The laws of the United States only extend to our country—so what happens if your work ends up in another country? Thanks to technology, and the Internet specifically, this happens all the time.

Speaking of the Internet, there are some great online resources that can complement what you've read in this book. We've briefly described a few key websites that will make sure you're up-to-date on all the latest and greatest with respect to copyrights.

We've given you a lot of information, but there will always be situations where it makes sense to enlist a lawyer to get you the rest of the way there. In this chapter, we give you helpful hints in choosing the right lawyer for your copyright needs.

Copyrights in Foreign Lands

There's really no such thing as an international copyright. Copyright is handled by the laws of each country individually. You're probably worried that many countries ignore copyright law so that book you're writing might show up in some faraway country, straight from the copy shop. Actually, that's not true. Much effort has been made to develop international treaties to protect the works of residents of those countries. A treaty is essentially an agreement between countries (rather than a law that applies to multiple countries). People in most countries have the same fear as Americans do when it comes to copying a work that has taken a significant amount of time to develop.

The Berne Convention

One international treaty is known as The Berne Convention. It became effective for the United States on March 1, 1989. The Berne Convention provides for the protection of copyrights internationally, without registration in those countries. Because the United States is a member of this treaty, you will receive what is called *national treatment* under The Berne Convention. If your copyrighted work is

infringed in a country that is a member of The
Berne Convention, national treatment permits you
to take action as if you were a citizen of that country. It is based on the general belief that countries
take care of their own citizens, but they don't take
care of foreigners. All member territories are equal-
ized under The Berne Convention.

For example, say you registered your book in the
United States and someone in Germany made copies
of your book and started distributing it in German
bookstores. You would be able to pursue a German
infringement action against the infringer in Germany
as if you were a German citizen.

The Universal Copyright Convention

In addition to The Berne Convention, there is one
other important international treaty related to copyrights. It is known as the Universal Copyright
Convention (UCC).

The UCC simplifies formality requirements related
to copyrights for countries that have signed up to
the UCC. Here's an example. If a member country
requires some fancy copyright notice to be put on
your copyrighted work three times per page, the
UCC eliminates that requirement and instead you
can simply put the © symbol next to the year of
first publication and the name of the copyright owner
(example: © 1996 Lizabeth Michaels). The only
positioning requirement is that the notice needs to
be in an obvious place so that someone reviewing
the work would have "reasonable notice" of your
copyright claim. Oftentimes, copyright notice is

located early in a book or at the bottom of a stand-alone (single-page) piece.

Other International Protections

There are a few more protections afforded under international law that you should be aware of:

- **Two-way agreements between the United States and another country.** Oftentimes, these exist instead of a treaty among several countries.

- **WIPO Copyright Treaty.** This protects works in a digital format.

- **WIPO Performances and Phonograms.** This is also known under the popular name of Geneva Convention and focuses on protecting sound recording works from piracy.

Be Careful in Certain Countries

Despite the advances made under the Berne Convention, the UCC and other treaties, there are still some benefits to copyright registration in individual countries. In many of the member countries, country specific registration can allow you to enjoy assumed validity of your copyright as well as seek awards for statutory damages and attorneys' fees.

Don't Make Assumptions

Remember that not every country has signed up to these treaties. In some countries your protection will be limited or there won't be any protection at all for your works. If you are concerned about the protection of your work in a particular foreign country, you should research that country to ensure that the Berne Convention and the UCC or other laws apply. For example, China is a notable exception to the countries that signed on to The Berne Convention. And here's a tip: Consider avoiding publication of the work until after you've confirmed these foreign laws since publication often impacts the manner in which foreign law is applied.

Online Copyright Resources

There are many websites that will provide you with excellent additional information regarding copyrights—in the United States and abroad. Of course, you can always mail or e-mail us—the authors—should you have any questions and we'll be pleased to point you in the right direction. Also, we provide a variety of resources, including a periodic electronic newsletter that you can sign up for through our website at www.lavagroup.net.

The Mother of Copyright Websites

The official website of the Registrar of Copyrights (the U.S. Copyright Office) is www.copyright.gov. From this site, you will be able to access all of the registration forms that are needed. This website also provides you with a variety of resources and circulars that are published by the U.S. Copyright Office. These circulars often contain analysis and descriptions of changes to the copyright laws as well as interpretations of specific regulations. Because these circulars are published by the U.S. Copyright Office, they have a high degree of reliability (as opposed to some outside person's interpretation of the law).

Another important feature is the search component. From www.copyright.gov, you're able to search records of registration and ownership going back to 1978. Although it is a useful feature, it's sometimes difficult to locate specific records if you don't know the name of the person who owns the copyright or if you're not sure of the work's title. You may recall from our earlier discussion: It's important to name works appropriately so they can be found later!

The Copyright Clearance Center

The Copyright Clearance Center (www.copyright. com), CCC for short, is the largest licensor of text reproduction rights in the world. Nearly 10,000 publishers and hundreds of thousands of authors utilize the CCC to license their works. These works are licensed to a variety of businesses and nonprofit organizations such as universities, law firms, government agencies, and many large corporations.

When would you use this service?

If you create an article or other work that others may want to reproduce, it is often easier to allow the CCC to manage the rights to use your work through their long-standing licensing program. Simply go to the CCC's website and click the tab for author and creator services.

If you're interested in licensing a work that is licensed through the CCC, the CCC's website provides an easy way to enter into a licensing relationship. This approach ensures that you are not infringing someone else's copyrighted work.

World Intellectual Property Organization

The World Intellectual Property Organization (www.wipo.org) is one of the specialized units of the United Nations and focuses on enforcing 23 international treaties related to intellectual property (including The Berne Convention and the Universal Copyright Convention). The WIPO extends beyond copyrights to other forms of intellectual property, such as patents and trademarks.

ASCAP and BMI

As you've read in Chapter 9, ASCAP (www.ascap.com) and BMI (www.bmi.com) provide blanket licenses to a variety of published music titles. Together, these organizations protect the works of hundreds of thousands of U.S. composers, songwriters, lyricists, and music publishers, and many more international individuals. These organizations also hand our royalty payments to composers for the works they license. The organization was formed to simplify the overall approach to getting permission to play music (Just imagine going to thousands of song writers yourself!).

(The Motion Picture Licensing Corporation (MPLC)

The MPLC (www.mplc.com) grants organizations that are licensed the right to show their video cassette and DVD content to nonprofit groups, government organizations, and businesses. This is done through an umbrella license—you don't need an individual license for each movie; the license covers their whole library. The MPLC has about 100,000 licensed facilities.

Using an Attorney

We mentioned earlier in this book that it might not be necessary to use an attorney for registering a copyright with the U.S. Copyright Office. When it comes to matters such as infringement or licensing of a copyright, using an attorney is often useful, if not critical. With respect to copyright registration, there are still some reasons to use an attorney. Therefore, we want to take you through some of the benefits of using an attorney in your copyright matters.

- **Greater assurances.** While the information in this book should get you through the copyright registration process as well as introduce you to a variety of other important issues and considerations, it's always good to have someone who is an expert on copyright issues. If you do not hire an attorney to take care of a copyright matter (registration, for example), you can at least request a quick review to make sure you did everything properly. This should not cost too much and may give you the added assurance you need.

- **"Safehouse" for your registration records.** For copyright registrations, your attorney likely maintains organized files including the correspondence sent to and received from the Copyright Office, a copy of your registration notice (with your registration number) and any communications between you and the Office (which can be helpful if there's ever a dispute as to who developed the copyrighted work).

- **Involvement in related matters.** Oftentimes, the process of copyrighting a work or dealing with another copyright issue is only one part of a much larger effort you're undertaking (for example, copyrighting a software program may also be related to forming a company, entering into a contract for services, and so on). If this is the case, it is probably a good idea to have an attorney assist you in the overall process to ensure that you fully understand your rights and obligations.

Picking an Attorney

Choosing the right attorney for your copyright matter really depends on a variety of matters and what you believe you'll need from the attorney in the long run.

References

In every service profession there are good, okay, and downright bad professionals. With respect to intellectual property professionals, this rule holds true. Therefore, it is important that you do your homework and select an attorney who has *demonstrated* the ability to handle the work you will ask him or her to do. The best way to do this is to obtain a referral from someone you trust who has worked with an attorney in the past on a related matter. In the absence of a personal referral, you should ask the attorney for two or three references.

In addition to references, you should ask the attorney questions related to each of the other topics in this section (time, cost, experience in a related matter, and personality).

Time

One of the biggest complaints about attorneys is their responsiveness to a client's needs. Failure to handle a client's request in a timely manner is usually because of the lawyer's busy schedule. Therefore, you should reach agreement on the exact information that the lawyer needs from you and the time frame for filing once the information is submitted. Then, hold him or her to it. The same applies for any other tasks that you may request of the lawyer.

Straight from the Record

Did you know that most states have a bar rule specifically focused on attorney response time to client requests? The state bar rules often require "prompt" compliance with reasonable requests for information from the client.

Experience in Related Matters

As we stated earlier, a copyright issue may be part of a larger effort you are undertaking, such as launching a business. You may also have other forms of intellectual property you want to protect (such as patents or trademarks). If this is the case, you may need more specialized knowledge in the area of intellectual property. There are many attorneys who, either individually or through their law firm, can provide a full array of intellectual property services. If you believe a copyright is the only type of intellectual property protection you will seek and you are forming a new business or have other ongoing legal needs related to your business, you should make sure that the lawyer, or the firm at which he or she practices, handles this type of corporate transactional work. To ensure that the attorney handling your copyright registration is qualified, you should ask the attorney specific questions regarding his or her experiences.

Personality Fit

One item that is often overlooked is the personality fit between the client and the attorney. Many people possess preconceived notions about the personalities of attorneys. They're tough, over-opinionated, nerdy, sarcastic, introverted, extroverted, or worse! In reality, there are different personalities of lawyers and you can find one that fits your unique needs. Most important, you should feel comfortable to approach and discuss any matter with your attorney and know that he or she will respond to you in a quick and informative way.

Straight from the Record

Lawyers can be a big help but have also caused clients great frustration over the years, hence the category of jokes known as lawyer jokes. A Google search for lawyer jokes uncovered 162,000 hits!

Cost

The most important item to a client is typically the cost of an attorney. It is also likely the reason for many individuals wanting to file their own copyright registrations. Please make sure you consider the other factors and benefits described above.

That being said, you should request a flat fee for registration of your copyright and should expect this fee to be relatively reasonable. Our research shows that attorneys charge from $200 to $600 to register an individual copyright.

The Least You Need to Know

- Check to make sure that your work is protected in all countries that you care about.

- There are many great online resources to increase your knowledge about copyrights and keep you up-to-date on any changes.

- It is often helpful to utilize an attorney on your copyright matters.

Further Readings

Chused, Richard H. *A Copyright Anthology: The Technology Frontier.* Ottawa, Ontario: Anderson Publishing, 1998.

Fishman, Stephen. *Copyright Your Software.* Third Edition. California: Nolo Press, 2001.

———. *The Public Domain: How to Find Copyright-Free Writings, Music, Art & More.* Second Edition. California: Nolo Press, 2004.

Geller, Paul Edward. Ed. *International Copyright Law and Practice.* United Kingdom: Oxford University Press, 1994.

Isenberg, Doug. *GigaLaw Guide to Internet Law.* New York: Random House Trade Paperbacks, 2002.

Leaffer, Marshall A. *Understanding Copyright Law.* Third Edition. New York: Matthew Bender & Company, 1999.

Menn, Joseph. *All the Rave: The Rise and Fall of Shawn Fanning's Napster.* New York: Crown Business, 2003.

Nimmer, Melville B. and David Nimmer. *Nimmer on Copyright.* New York: Matthew Bender & Company, 2004.

Samuels, Edward. *The Illustrated Story of Copyright.* New York: St. Martin's Press, 2000.

Stim, Richard. *Getting Permission: How to License and Clear Copyrighted Materials Online and Off.* California: Nolo Press, 1999.

Glossary

access   Refers to whether a person could have seen a copyrighted work that they are accused of infringing on.

adaptation   A transformation of a work into another form, such as creating a film version of a favorite book.

assignment   The sale of something to another person.

collective work   A collection of individual pieces and works that make up a final product.

compilation   A group of information put together in such a way that the final product as a whole can be considered original and creative.

copyright   A legal form of protection for original works of authorship that have been fixed into a physical form.

copyright infringement   When you reproduce, adapt, display, perform, or distribute someone else's copyrighted work.

display   Includes showing a copy via TV, film, or any other device or method.

distribution　The selling or renting of a protected work to others.

expression　The unique way in which you present information, perform a play, write a song, or provide your opinion on a topic.

fixed in a tangible medium　When a work is placed into a form that can be perceived or communicated by others.

HTML　Short for Hyper Text Mark-up Language, a system for marking up a document so it can be published to the World Wide Web and displayed in a web browser.

infringement　An action, such as copying or reproducing, that is in direct violation of the rights granted under copyright law.

intellectual property　Creations of the mind that can be protected by law, bought, sold, traded, rented, and sued over.

license　An agreement to rent something, such as a copyright, to another person.

literary works　Expressions in words, numbers, or other verbal manners that are recorded in a physical form.

notice　Refers to making others aware that your work is protected under copyright law and typically includes the word *copyright* or the copyright symbol (©) along with the date of publication.

online work　Information presented online, for example on the home page of a website.

patents   A form of legal protection for ideas, inventions, processes, and methods; they are not copyrights.

performance   Includes reciting, rendering, playing, dancing, and acting.

performing arts works   Works that are intended to be performed in front of an audience (either live, or through a device like a TV, or in a movie theatre).

piracy   Refers to the act of illegally copying and/or selling software products.

publication   When a work is copied and distributed to the public.

registration   Refers to the process of filing a work to by copyrighted with the copyright office.

recordation   The process of fixing a work in a tangible medium.

reproduction   Making copies of a copyrighted work; only the copyright owner has the right to reproduce the work.

serials   Works intended to be issued in successive parts with a serial number on each issue, such as a monthly magazine with the month and year on the cover.

substantial similarity   Occurs if the average person would conclude that an alleged infringing work has incorporated important parts of another work.

software   Is the expression of a computer programmer's idea for a program that runs on a computing device.

sound recordings   Works that have a series of spoken, musical, or other types of sounds.

trademarks   A form of legal protection for words and symbols that help consumers identify the origin of goods.

visual arts works   Include paintings, sculptures, drawings, jewelry designs and dolls.

works   Items that are created by an author; for example, books, poems, pictures, or the like.

Index

P-Q

Y–Z

The only pocket-sized guides for writers, composers, inventors, web masters, designers, and other creators to focus in on the ever-changing and complex world of patents, copyrights, and trademarks.

The Pocket Idiot's Guide™ to Copyrights
ISBN: 1-59257-228-6
$9.95

The Pocket Idiot's Guide™ to Trademarks
ISBN: 1-59257-230-8
$9.95

The Pocket Idiot's Guide™ to Patents
ISBN: 1-59257-229-4
$9.95

- ◆ Written by expert attorneys in the field
- ◆ Presented in clear, layperson's language
- ◆ Explores everything from the origins and theories to the most effective ways to file for a copyright, patent, or trademark
- ◆ Includes helpful examples of government filing documents
- ◆ Contains helpful Internet and government resource guides